Adulting Hard for Young Women

Essential Life Skills to Become Independent, Wealthy, Healthier, Happier, and Generally a More Interesting Woman in Your Early Twenties

Jeffrey C. Chapman

CONTENTS

To my beloved daughter, Danielle,

Thank you for your unwavering support and invaluable contributions throughout the writing of this book. Your objective feminine perspective has helped to shape my ideas and insights in ways that I could not have achieved on my own. I am immensely grateful for the time and effort you have devoted to this project.

Your honesty and critical feedback have been instrumental in making this book the best it could be. Your keen eye for detail, coupled with your unique perspective, has helped to ensure that every aspect of this work is well-researched, well-reasoned, and engaging for all readers.

Most importantly, I want you to know how proud I am of the person you have become. Your intelligence, creativity, and strength of character inspire me every day, and I feel so fortunate to have you as my daughter. I hope that this book serves as a testament to our special bond and the incredible teamwork we share.

Thank you for being an amazing daughter, and for always reminding me that I'm a "cool dad" (even when I may not feel like it). I love you more than words can express.

INTRODUCTION

Ready to take on the real world and finally become an "adult"? Well, you can pass on the boring lectures your parents gave you as a kid about responsibility—from budgeting like a pro to making more mature decisions, adulting doesn't have to be so serious. This book provides young women like you with all of the tips, tricks, and advice for taking charge of their lives in an empowering way, because, let's be honest, growing up is hard enough without having to feel restricted by our elders!

For young women, adulting can be scary, especially if they have to take care of all parts of their lives for the first time. Things like learning how to cook, cleaning and fixing stuff around the house, buying a car and negotiating a great deal, understanding health insurance, learning how to budget and invest hard-earned money, finding a career path, navigating relationships with family and friends, and so much more! Just thinking about it is enough to make anyone's head spin!

But there is no need to fear; adulting doesn't have to be overwhelming or intimidating. As you get older and become an adult, you need to find ways to give yourself more power while also taking care of your physical, emotional, and financial health. This book will give you the tools you need to do just that! You'll learn how to shop smartly for groceries, understand what kind of health coverage is right for you, manage your finances responsibly, create an emergency fund, and even find a life partner. With practical advice on these topics and more, Adulting Hard will help you take charge of your future with confidence.

I've always been a bit of a control freak, so when my kids moved out of the house, it was hard for me to let them go. I mean, who was going to beg them to clean their room? Who would make sure they did their laundry and stayed on top of their bills? Who else could order takeout food like I do every Friday night? It was clear that my kids were going to have to learn some basic life skills if they wanted to survive in adulthood, and luckily, I had just enough knowledge myself (or at least access to Google) to help guide them through.

I'm not going to lie, teaching them all these adulting basics wasn't easy, but once they got the hang of it, they didn't want to stop—and now they know more than me. But hey, at least now I can brag about how much more mature my children are than me! And besides...it's kind of nice having an excuse when someone asks why you don't know how to do something. "Oh sorry, but you see...my children haven't taught me yet!"

At least my kids now know how to not just survive but actually thrive in adulthood—and that's all thanks to me! (Just kidding...but seriously, I'm proud of them). Now, if only I could get them to remember that all the hard work was worth it and to come home to visit every now and then. Ah well, one day at a time. :)

Adulting is not something one achieves by turning a certain age. It's a state of mind. It's learning how to do things like an adult.

I'm not sure how I survived all these years without learning how to do the things mentioned above. Growing up, I was never much of a home improvement person or a good cook. Fast food and takeout were my staples. During the pandemic, however, I realized that if I wanted to get by, I would have to learn how to do these things. So I watched YouTube tutorials, read books, and asked my friends who are experts in their respective fields for advice.

To my surprise, I found that adulting wasn't as hard as I had thought. Sure it took some practice, but with a bit of patience and determination, I was able to tackle all the projects I set out to do. In the end, I was able to improve my home and even whip up a few delicious meals for my family. So if you're ever feeling overwhelmed by adulting, take a deep breath and remember that it's never too late to learn something new! Who knows, maybe you'll find that with a bit of effort, you too can be a successful adult. Good luck!

CHAPTER ONE

YOU'RE ON YOUR OWN... NOW WHAT?

L IVING ALONE FOR THE first time can be an exciting yet daunting experience. From finding the perfect place to call home to managing your finances and other responsibilities, there are a lot of things to consider as you make this life transition. Whether you're looking for a roommate or planning on living alone, it can be overwhelming trying to figure out where to start.

In this chapter, we will explore some of the pros and cons of living alone versus having a roommate, as well as tips on how to find the right place for your needs and budget. I'll also give you tips on how to get ready to rent your own place so that you can feel confident that you've made an informed choice about your future home. We'll also discuss ways to protect your deposit, provide helpful home maintenance and repair tips, and offer some basic decorating ideas.

So take a deep breath, and let's get started on your journey to find a perfect place of your own!

• • • ● • ● • • •

Finding the Perfect Place to Live: Tips for New Renters

The first thing to consider when looking for a place of your own is how much space you need and what type of living situation would suit you best. Do you prefer a house, an apartment, or a condo? Are you looking for something more modern or traditional? These are all important questions to consider when finding the perfect place to call home.

Finding the right place to rent can be a daunting task. There are many steps involved in renting a place, from making sure you have all of the necessary paperwork to understanding what type of rental agreement you're signing and ensuring your application is approved. It's important to understand the process thoroughly so that you don't get taken advantage of or end up paying more than necessary. We'll go over some key tips for navigating the rental process, such as how to create an effective renter profile and how renters insurance works. We'll also go over other important things like how to carefully read a lease before signing it and what your rights are as a renter. With these tips in mind, you should feel confident that your search will help you find just the right home for your needs!

These are some of the questions to ask yourself when looking for a place to live:

- Are there any great take-out restaurants nearby?

- Does the neighborhood have a good safety record?

- Is it easy to find parking in the area?

- What kind of public transportation is available?

- How close are grocery stores and other essential services?

- Can I get a gym membership within walking distance from my apartment or house?

- Is the area noisy during certain hours of the day or night, like early morning for example, due to traffic noise, construction, etc.?

- Are there any parks or green spaces nearby that offer outdoor activities such as hiking trails, biking paths, dog runs, etc.?

- Are there any local attractions or events nearby?

- What kind of community activities and programs are available in the area?

- Is this a pet-friendly building/neighborhood?

- Does the landlord require a credit check before approving my application?

- Do I need to pay an additional security deposit if I bring a pet with me?

- How long will it take to get approved for renting this property?

- Are there any restrictions on when or how often I can have visitors stay over at my place?

- Is it possible to sublet the apartment if I plan on traveling for some time away from home and don't want to terminate the lease agreement early?

Bonus tip: Never sign a lease for a place you haven't seen in person. It's always best to visit the property and make sure it meets your expectations before committing to a long-term rental agreement! And before even visiting a place, make sure you go on Google Maps and use the "Street" feature to do a virtual tour of the neighborhood.

• • • ● • ● • • •

Pros and Cons of Living Alone vs. Having a Roommate

Next are the considerations of living alone versus having a roommate. Of course, it's easier on the wallet to have a roommate and split the costs, but there are many other things to consider as well. Are you comfortable having someone else in your space? Will you be able to work out how the bills will be paid? Can you handle the responsibility of signing a lease on your own without anyone else's help?

These are some pros and cons of living on your own:

Pros:

- More privacy and independence

- No need to compromise with a roommate

- Ability to decorate as desired without needing approval from another person

- Being able to do things your own way without having any conflicts

Cons:

- It can become lonely with no one to talk or interact with regularly

- Higher bills since you have to pay for everything yourself

- More responsibility and maintenance tasks that can't be shared (such as cleaning, repairs, etc.)

- Limited resources: if you encounter an emergency situation, there may not be anyone around who could help you

How about living with one or more roommates?

Pros:

- Shared costs of rent and bills, making it easier to afford

- Companionship and support with day-to-day tasks

- Someone to talk to if you're feeling lonely or down

- Often more enjoyable than living alone as there is someone around for social activities

Cons:

- Inadequate privacy: You may overhear conversations or arguments between roommates that you would not have heard if you lived alone

- Differing lifestyles can cause conflict; one roommate might like things clean while another might be less tidy

- Roommates often bring their friends over, which could limit your quiet time at home

- Financial responsibilities may end up being unequal, leaving one person shouldering the majority of the burden

Living with good friends or complete strangers can be an exciting and rewarding experience. For some, having a roommate can provide companionship and camaraderie that simply aren't available when living alone. But for others, living with a stranger can be overwhelming; it's important to know what to expect before committing to such an arrangement.

Finding the right roommate can be a challenging yet rewarding experience. Finding and choosing a roommate is a multi-step process that includes researching possible candidates, meeting with them, and then making a choice. Getting to know each step can help you make the best choice for yourself and your new living situation.

Before beginning the process of looking for a roommate, it is important to understand what qualities you would like to see in a potential roommate. This can include things such as pets, relationships, morning and night routines, social life, vices, music and movie tastes, preferred tasks and chores around the house, personality type (introvert or extrovert), cleanliness and organizational preferences, and future plans.

Once you have your list of criteria for a potential roommate, it is time to start the interview process. This includes researching candidates online or through word-of-mouth referrals, asking questions about the qualities mentioned in the previous step during interviews, and making sure that both parties sign a written agreement that spells out expectations and responsibilities.

Here are some questions you might ask a potential roommate:

- How do you take your coffee?

- Do you like cats or dogs better?

- Which household chores are your forte, and what do you dread doing the most?

- If you could describe yourself in three words, which ones would they be?

- If a pizza delivery person showed up at our door right now, what toppings would you get?

- Are unicorns real or just a myth?

- What's your spirit animal?

- What is the weirdest thing that has ever happened to you while traveling abroad?

- What do you do to de-stress after a long day?

- If you could live anywhere in the world, where would it be and why?

- What kind of music do you like to listen to when no one is around?

- Are you into doing DIY projects, or do you prefer taking the easy way out?

- Would you say that your creative or logical side dominates?

- Do you have any allergies or special dietary requirements?

- Are you comfortable cooking meals with your roommate(s)?

- Are there any items that you would like to keep off-limits?

- How do you handle disagreements with roommates?

- What do you think is the biggest challenge when it comes to living together in a shared space?

- Will anyone else be living with us besides yourself, and if so, how many people can we expect at any given time?

- Are friends welcome to come by anytime, or do you want advance notice?

- What hobbies or activities take up most of your free time when not working or studying?

- Are there certain hours during which noise should be kept to a minimum (such as studying, sleeping, etc.)?

- What is your stance on drug use?

- Are you currently in a relationship?

- How would you describe your sexual orientation (straight, gay, lesbian, bi)?

- Do you think society should respect and accept people with different sexual and romantic preferences?

- How long do you anticipate living together?

- What would be your ideal timeline for moving out?

- Do you want to stay in this area long term or relocate somewhere else?

- Do you have any plans to move in the near future, either temporarily or permanently?

- Are you looking for a short-term rental arrangement or a longer commitment of at least two years?

- Are you interested in exploring different neighborhoods and cities with your roommate, if it's affordable?

At the end of the day, finding a roommate is a lot like dating. It's important to take your time, ask lots of questions, and make sure that you are comfortable with the person and the living arrangements. With a little patience, thoughtfulness, and an open mind, you will be able to find a roommate who is the perfect fit for your lifestyle!

Renting a place can be an exciting and nerve-wracking experience. The application process can be particularly overwhelming, especially for new renters. After all, your future landlord will be judging your character based on what you include in the application—everything from your credit score to your employment history and even references. But don't let that scare you away from a great opportunity! With the right know-how, you can make sure that your application stands out among the rest.

When you're a first-time renter and don't have enough good credit, there are a few steps you can take to increase your chances of getting approved for an apartment. One of the most important things to do is establish a renter's profile.

A renter's profile is an important part of the application process that can save time and ensure you get the rental approval you're looking for. This profile is basically a summary or overview of all the information landlords look for when deciding whether or not to rent to a person. This includes identification, credit score, criminal history, employment history, references, income verification, current address, and more. It can be an overwhelming task to compile all this information in one place, so a renter's profile is a great way to save yourself the trouble.

Renters insurance is also a must-have when finding and securing your new place, but it's something that many people overlook when searching for an apartment. It's important to understand what it is and why it's so crucial to get coverage. It's usually not very expensive and provides financial protection in case of unforeseen circumstances such as property damage or theft. It will also cover any liability costs should someone be injured while on the premises.

The lease agreement is another integral part of renting a place. Before signing anything, make sure you have thoroughly read it and understand what each clause means. Be aware of your rights as a tenant, such as the right to terminate the lease with proper notice. Be sure to also look out for any hidden costs or surprise fees that may be included in the agreement.

Renters have certain rights that are protected by law. New renters should learn about these rights so that they don't get taken advantage of. A landlord can't treat people differently because of their race, religion, gender identity, or sexual orientation. This is one of the most important rights. They must also abide by fair housing laws and provide safe, livable conditions.

Finding the right place to rent can be time-consuming, but with thorough research and preparation, you should have no trouble getting approved. Don't forget to compile your renter's profile, get renter's insurance, read the lease agreement carefully, and know your rights before signing off on anything!

• • • ● • ● • • •

So you've moved in. What's next?

Now that you've moved into your new place, it's time to make sure all of your utilities and services are in order. The first step is to research all of the different utilities available in your area, such as electricity, gas, water, cable, and the internet. Once you have identified which ones you may need for your new home, it's time to start signing up and getting them connected.

Unless you live in a building that includes all of the necessary utilities, you'll need to do some extra legwork and contact each provider individually. Don't forget about those little extras either, such as recycling and waste removal services!

Once your utilities are sorted, don't forget to update your address in all the relevant places. This includes everything from changing it for credit cards, banks, and insurance companies to updating your driver's license and registering to vote in your new area.

Oh, and one last thing: don't forget to sign up for mail forwarding! It's a great way to ensure that you don't miss out on anything important from your old address.

Moving house is a big change, but with the right preparation, it can be a smooth and simple process.

• • • ● • ● • • •

It's your place; now make it your own.

Once you have all of your utilities sorted out and your address updated, it's time to make your new place feel like home. The best way to do this is by adding some cozy touches that create a sense of warmth and comfort.

To start, you could hang up some string lights around the edges of the room and bring in some furniture. Adding some throw pillows and a blanket will also help to make the room feel more inviting. From there, you can start painting, adding artwork and pictures, and hanging shelves to showcase your favorite books or knick-knacks—whatever makes you comfortable!

Remember, it's your place and your space, so do what feels right. Make it a place you want to come home to and enjoy!

Make sure you read your lease agreement to find out if you should leave the place the way you found it and to see how much it would cost you if the landlord had to fix it when you left. It's also a good idea to take a few pictures of the place when you first move in and compare them to when you leave, just to prove that any damages were there before you moved in. If you're allowed to hang things up, be sure to use appropriate hardware such as anchors or wall plugs, unless your landlord is okay with holes being drilled. And if you plan on painting, that can be a great way to make your new place feel like home. Just remember to get permission from the landlord first and consider repainting the place back to its original state when you move out.

No matter what changes you decide to make in your new place, it's important for you to know what you can and cannot do in terms of decorating. Understanding the rules of your lease agreement will help ensure that you don't get into any trouble with the landlord.

Here are 20 great and inexpensive decorating ideas for your new place:

1. Brighten up your walls with a fresh coat of paint in light, calming colors.

2. Add some personality to the room by incorporating wall art and decorations like posters, mirrors, or framed photographs.

3. Draw attention to certain areas with accent lighting (you can find good quality lamps on sale at home improvement stores).

4. Change out your window treatments for something more impactful; think of roman shades, curtains, or blinds.

5. Give furniture an upgrade with slipcovers or new cushions for a comfy look and feel.

6. Make use of vertical space by adding shelves and bookcases to store books/items away neatly.

7. Try sprucing up old furniture pieces by refinishing them with different paints or stains.

8. Find stylish items at thrift shops, flea markets, or online secondhand stores.

9. Use area rugs strategically around the room—this is a great way to make it seem bigger than it actually is.

10. Bring life into the apartment with plants (real ones are best but you can also opt for artificial greenery).

11. Hang a gallery wall of your favorite photos or art pieces to make it more person-

alized.

12. Use creative storage solutions like baskets, cubbies, or hanging organizers.

13. Add texture and depth with textured rugs, throws, and pillows.

14. Incorporate multi-functional furniture items such as daybeds for seating during the day and sleeping at night.

15. Take advantage of natural light—open up curtains/shades to let the sunshine in whenever possible.

16. Try setting up an outdoor living space with comfortable chairs/sofas where you can relax outdoors when the weather permits.

17. Don't be afraid of bold colors—add some bright hues with accent walls, furniture pieces, or decorative accessories.

18. Have fun mixing different patterns together, but remember not to go overboard; two patterns are usually enough.

19. Install floating shelves on unused wall spaces or corners for extra storage options while saving floor space.

20. Create a cozy "nook" area by arranging several cushions in one corner.

With these easy and affordable decorating ideas, you can make your new place feel cozy and inviting in no time! So don't be afraid to get creative—have fun with it!

When I was in the process of remodeling our 20+-year-old kitchen, I did a lot of research on Pinterest. I had no idea how to decorate a room, let alone an entire kitchen; however, looking at what people who knew what they were doing did to their spaces allowed me to be more daring and fearless myself.

See? Adulting is a state of mind!

Protecting Your Deposit: How to Do Basic Repairs and Home Maintenance

It's time to roll up your sleeves and get down to business! In this section, you'll learn how to do basic repairs and home maintenance in no time. Whether it's unclogging a toilet, hanging pictures and shelves, patching holes in the walls, clearing clogged drains, painting walls, cleaning bathroom surfaces and floors, or even doing dishes efficiently and properly, I've got you covered. Also included are recommendations for tools that every woman should own for home repairs and maintenance, as well as cleaning supplies that should be kept on hand at all times. So let's get started!

How to unclog the toilet

 We've all been there: You flush the toilet, and nothing happens. The water just keeps rising higher and higher until you start to worry that it's going to spill out over the top. It's an emergency situation, but don't panic! Unclogging a toilet is not as difficult or intimidating as it may seem. In fact, with a few simple steps and some elbow grease (and maybe a plunger), you'll be able to get your toilet running like new in no time! So let's take a look at how to unclog that pesky commode once and for all.

Using a plunger:

If your toilet won't flush, don't be scared. 9 times out of 10, it can be fixed with a simple plunger! Here are some tips on how to use it effectively:

1. Make sure the plunger is submerged in water before you start plunging.

2.

Move the plunger up and down with steady, forceful strokes until the clog starts to move or break apart.

3. Once you feel resistance while pushing down on the handle of the plunger, step back and wait for a few seconds to see if it had any effect before continuing.

4. If necessary, add some hot water to raise the level so that water covers most of the suction cup at all times while plunging.

5. After each plunge stroke, check whether there's been any improvement in terms of draining speed or the complete disappearance of standing water from the bowl.

6. When you finish unclogging, ensure that your toilet flushes correctly by running multiple "test flushes."

7. Make sure not to flush anything other than human waste and toilet paper after unclogging. Otherwise, you risk recurrence.

If plunging doesn't work, you can try using a snake or auger to reach further down into the pipe and break up any clogs that might be there.

Using a snake or auger:

A snake or auger is a tool that can reach deep into a pipe to break up clogs. Here are some tips on how to use one.

1. Wear gloves and safety glasses when handling the auger, as it can be sharp in places.

2. Make sure to check for any obstructions before inserting the auger into the drain pipe.

3. Rotate clockwise to break up any clogs or debris that might be stuck inside the pipe.

4. Start by pushing gently until you feel resistance, then increase pressure gradually while rotating clockwise until the clog is released.

5. Do not force if there is too much resistance—this may damage pipes or cause injuries.

6. If necessary, loosen the set screw on the handle of the auger and push down firmly on the opposite side of the handle so that the snake wire goes further down into the drainpipe.

7. When finished clearing out the pipe, run multiple "test flushes" with water from a bucket/container just outside the toilet bowl entrance.

8. Keep the plastic guard around the tip of the wire at all times during usage for safety purposes.

9. Dispose of it properly after use.

Using a chemical drain cleaner:

Finally, you may need to use a chemical cleaner like bleach or vinegar to get rid of stubborn clogs.

With these steps, you should be able to unclog your toilet in no time!

1. Wear rubber gloves when handling any type of chemical cleaner or toilet bowl cleaner, as some may be toxic and/or irritating if it comes in contact with skin.

2. Avoid mixing chemical cleaners together, as this can create dangerous chemical compounds that can damage your plumbing system or harm anyone who breathes them in directly from fumes or other forms of contact (such as splash-back).

3. Read all instructions carefully before beginning work so you understand how much of each product needs to be used, how long it should stay in the pipes

before being flushed away, etc.

4. Have plenty of ventilation available while you work (open windows and turn on fans if possible) so that fumes don't remain concentrated inside the bathroom area for too long, which could potentially cause health issues when inhaled over time or immediate irritation upon direct contact with skin or eyes, etc.

5. Finally, discard any remaining chemical cleaners according to manufacturer guidelines once finished—never pour anything down the drain.

If none of the three options above worked, I'm very sorry to inform you that you might need to call a plumber. What in the world did you try to flush down the toilet, an ex-boyfriend?

How to clear a clogged drain

 Every woman knows the frustration of a clogged drain—it's almost as if your sink is playing an evil game of hide-and-seek, and you just can't seem to find whatever is blocking the flow. But don't worry! With some simple steps, you'll be able to outsmart that pesky clog and have your sink back in action in no time. So grab your plunger, because here are some tips on how to clear a clogged drain like a pro!

1. Start by removing the drain stopper and cleaning out any debris or buildup.

2. If that doesn't work, use a plunger to dislodge the clog from the pipes.

3. For tougher clogs, pour ½ cup of baking soda followed by 1 cup of distilled white vinegar down the drain and cover with a wet cloth for 10 minutes to allow it to break down the blockage.

4. You can also try using chemical-based cleaners like Liquid Plumr or Drano, which contain caustic ingredients that will help dissolve whatever is causing your

drain to be blocked up in the first place.

5. Use an auger or "plumber's snake," which is essentially a long flexible metal wire with an attached handle on one end. Feed it into your pipe and crank gently until you feel resistance (hopefully this means you've reached what was blocking your pipes!), then pull back out slowly while loosening up anything stuck along its length—if done correctly, this should clear most common clogs!

6. Finally, if all else fails, resorting to professional plumbers may be necessary, but they are expensive, so make sure you try steps 1-5 before going down that road.

How to hang a picture or a shelf

Ah, putting up a picture or a shelf. It seems like such an easy task to do around the house—until you actually try and do it! Whether you're attempting to hang a heavy mirror in your bedroom or just trying to level out some shelves in your living room, this seemingly simple job can quickly turn into a headache if not done properly. But don't worry; with these tips and tricks, you'll master the art of wall decorating in no time! So grab your drill (or hammer!), and let's get started on making sure that your picture is perfectly hung. Just don't break any walls while doing so!

Hanging things requires anchors or fixings unless you are nailing directly on a wall stud. Otherwise, you risk tearing down the drywall.

1. Choose the right type of hardware for your wall surface: drywall anchor screws or plastic anchors for plaster/drywall, masonry (concrete) anchors for brick and concrete blocks, and toggle bolts for a hollow core door.

2. Mark the spot where you want to hang the picture or shelf with a pencil, making sure that it is level before drilling any holes into the wall.

3. Drill each hole for the hardware you've chosen a little deeper than what it says on the package to make sure there's enough room for all the anchor parts to fit

right when you put them in place later.

4. Insert the fixings into their respective holes using either a screwdriver or hammer, depending on which type of anchor you chose. Make sure they are flush against the wall once fitted because gaps can potentially cause damage over time due to movement when hanging items later down the line!

5. Hang up your picture/shelf by placing its two hooks onto either side of your chosen fixings—most pictures and shelves come with pre-drilled holes, but if not, then simply use appropriately sized screws (or nails!) instead. Just remember that heavier objects require more secure fixings such as toggle bolts!

6. Finally, use a level to make sure your item is straight and adjust any screws or anchors as necessary.

How to patch a hole in the wall

 Oh yeah! Patching holes in the wall. It's a task that almost all of us have had to do at some point or another. Whether you're moving out of an apartment and need to make sure it looks as good as new for the next tenant, or you just made a mistake while attempting DIY home improvements, chances are you'll encounter this problem! With these tips and tricks, I can help turn your wall from looking like Swiss cheese into something resembling a masterpiece! So grab your drill (or hammer!) and let's get started on patching up those pesky holes—hopefully without making any more in the process!

1. Start by preparing the area around the nail hole with a piece of medium grit sandpaper.

2. Wipe away any dust and debris from the surface using a damp cloth or sponge.

3. Fill the nail hole with spackle, using a putty knife to push it into place and level off any excess material on top of the wall's surface for an even finish.

4.

Allow the spackle to dry thoroughly; this may take up to 24 hours depending on how deep your original hole was, so be patient!

5. Once dry, lightly sand down any bumps or uneven patches that remain on your wall's surface until you achieve an even finish that looks like new again!

6. You can then paint over this patch if necessary; just make sure to use a primer first, which will help ensure maximum coverage and longevity when done correctly!

How to paint a wall

 Painting a wall can seem like a simple task, but it's easy to get carried away and end up with a bigger mess than you bargained for. Whether you're painting your own home or helping out a friend, here are some tips to help ensure that the only thing getting painted is the wall!

Gather the necessary materials before starting—this includes drop cloths, paint brushes or rollers, a paint tray, painter's tape, and of course, the actual paint!

2. Prepare the area by laying down a drop cloth to protect both your floors and ceiling from accidental splatters. Also, make sure all furniture has been covered properly with plastic sheeting if possible.

3. Use painter's tape along baseboards, corners, and edges to avoid painting any other surfaces that shouldn't be affected in the process (e.g., window sills).

4. Start at one corner of the wall and begin rolling outwards in even strokes until you reach the opposite side; use a brush on smaller areas as needed for precise coverage!

5. Cut in (or outline) around edges such as door/window frames or baseboards using a small angled brush for clean lines when transitioning between colors or

finishes—don't forget about any tight corners either!

6. Once finished painting, let it dry completely before touching up any spots you may have missed earlier on,no matter how tempted you are to take off those gloves now!

Tools Every Woman Should Own for Home Repairs & Maintenance

Having the right tools at home is essential for any woman to take care of repairs and maintenance. The following list will make your life a little easier and allow you to do basic repairs and maintenance on your own, but everything doesn't need to be purchased all at once; some items may already be around the house or can be bought piece by piece over time.

1. Hammer: A must-have for any repair job, be it a nail in the wall or building furniture.

2. Screwdriver set: An all-in-one is generally better than individual screwdrivers, as they come with multiple heads so you can quickly switch between different sizes and types.

3. Pliers

4. Tape measure: An essential tool for any homeowner, allowing you to quickly and easily measure out distances, angles, and curves. Whether you're planning a renovation project or simply trying to hang a picture, having a tape measure on hand can help make the job easier and more accurate. Tape measures are also surprisingly versatile; not only can they be used to measure walls, floors, and ceilings, but they can also be used to measure other materials such as fabric, wood, and even metal!

1. Utility Knife

2. Level Tool: This small tool will help you make sure everything is perfectly straight and aligned when hanging up pictures or shelves.

3. Wrench Set

4. Pipe Wrench: An essential tool for any woman who wants to take care of basic home repairs. A pipe wrench is a type of adjustable wrench that is specifically designed to grip and turn pipes, fittings, and other rounded surfaces. It has two jaws, one flat and one slightly curved, that can be adjusted by turning a screw mechanism on.

5. Hex Key/Allen Wrench Set: An Allen key set is a must-have for any home repair toolkit! This versatile tool consists of a number of small hexagonal keys that can be used to loosen and tighten screw heads, providing greater precision and torque than what can be achieved with more traditional tools. Additionally, these tools are incredibly lightweight and convenient.

6. Electric Drill

7. Sandpaper

8. Putty Knife

9. Stud Finder: An essential tool for any homeowner or DIY enthusiast. This nifty device uses magnetic, electronic, or ultrasound technology to locate metal and wooden studs behind walls and other structures, which can then be used for mounting shelves, hanging pictures, and more.

10. Extension Cords

11. Electric Multi-tool: A power multi-tool is a must-have for any home repair and maintenance DIYer. It can help you tackle difficult tasks with ease and accuracy in less time than it would take to use traditional tools. This versatile tool has several attachments that can be used for different jobs, such as cutting through materials like wood or metal. I bought mine during the pandemic, and I've used it for everything... It cuts like butter!

12.

Utility knife ("Swiss army knife")

13. Assorted screws (and their plastic fittings, a.k.a wall anchors)

14. Assorted nuts and bolts

15. Assorted nails

16. Extra light bulbs

17. Silicone sealant

18. Spackle (Filler)

19. Toolbox

20. Glue gun: A glue gun is an indispensable tool for home repairs and maintenance. It can be used for a variety of tasks from crafting to carpentry and is especially useful for quickly fixing broken items or making temporary repairs. A glue gun is easy to use and can save time and money compared to having to get things professionally repaired.

21. Safety goggles

22. Safety gloves

How to clean the bathroom and floors

Cleaning the bathroom, toilet, floors, and other surfaces can be a frustrating task for even the most experienced of housekeepers. But with a little bit of great music playing in the background and some helpful tips, it doesn't have to be such a chore! Grab your rubber gloves, and let's get started on making sure that you don't need to call in a roach exterminator after all—because we all know how embarrassing that would be!

1. Prep the area by removing all items from countertops, shelves, and floors.

2. Dust off of any surface before wiping it down with a damp cloth or sponge. Use an all-purpose cleaner for tougher areas.

3. For toilet cleaning, start by using a brush to loosen up stuck-on debris in the bowl and flush away any residue that's left behind afterward. Be sure to wear protective gloves while doing this!

4. Clean the surfaces with an appropriate disinfectant (e.g., bleach), and let it sit for 5 minutes (or longer, if needed) before rinsing off thoroughly with warm water afterward.

5. Wipe down floors starting at one corner of the room and work your way outwards to avoid missing spots—use a mop and/or broom depending on what kind of flooring you have!

6. Vacuum up any remaining dust particles or pet hair once done mopping so that everything looks good as new upon completion!

How to properly do the dishes (without a dishwasher)

If you've always had a dishwasher, you might be in for a surprise if your new place doesn't have one, and you have to wash dishes by hand for the first time. If so, then this section is for you! It's time to learn the ins and outs of washing your dishes without any help from modern technology. From finding the right tools to understanding the proper technique, here's everything you need to know about hand-washing your dishes. Get ready for an adventure that will have you laughing as much as it has you scrubbing. Let's get started!

1. Get the right tools: Gather a sponge, dish soap, a kitchen towel, and a basin filled with warm water before getting started.

2. Pre-rinse the dishes: Loosen up any stuck-on food or grease by pre-rinsing your dishes in hot water first.

3. Scrape off excess debris: For heavier duty debris, use a knife to scrape away any

remaining residue from plates or bowls before washing them manually.

4. Wash gently: Use circular motions with the sponge and warm soapy water to clean off dirt and germs, taking care to avoid damaging delicate items like wine glasses or fine china dinnerware sets.

5. Rinse thoroughly: To avoid cloudy glassware later, make sure you rinse everything completely until there are no soapy suds left behind!

6. Dry with care: Use a clean cloth kitchen towel to dry each item carefully as soon as they come out of the sink—this will help prevent streaks or spots on your beautiful dishes!

7. Store properly: Put all the dishes back in their respective places once they're fully dried for easy access later on!

Cleaning Supplies Every Woman Should Have

1. Sponges

2. Dish soap

3. Kitchen towels

4. Basins/buckets for cleaning and rinsing dishes

5. Dishwasher tablets and liquid (if you have a dishwasher)

6. An all-purpose cleaner (multi-surface cleaner)

7. Glass cleaners

8. Brooms and dustpans to sweep up messes

9. A duster

10. Disinfectants such as Lysol wipes or liquid spray

11. A mop

12. A bucket

13. Rubber gloves (optional)

14. A vacuum cleaner

15. Laundry detergent

16. Fabric softener

17. Stain remover

18. A clothes rack if you don't have an external clothesline or dryer

19. Clothes hamper

20. Dryer sheets

21. A glass cleaner for the shower and mirrors

22. Fragrance for the bathroom

23. Bathroom towels

24. Bathroom mats

25. Toilet bowl cleaner

26. A plunger

27. A toilet brush

28. Trash cans

What to buy in bulk whenever you have a chance

We all know that buying in bulk is often the cheapest way to shop, especially for those items that don't go bad and you'll always need more of. Toilet paper is a great example of this. Why do we buy it by the case or even multiple cases when one roll will last us several days? Well, because unless you know something I don't, you will probably need toilet paper for the rest of your life.

Some items make sense to buy in bulk, such as:

1. Toilet Paper

2. Paper Towels

3. Laundry Detergent

4. Fabric Softener

5. Dishwashing Liquid/Tablets

6. Cleaning Supplies (all-purpose cleaners, glass cleaners, etc)

7. Garbage Bags

8. Lightbulbs/Batteries

9. Hand Soap Dispenser Refills

10. Pet Food and Treats

11. Food Bags (Ziploc style)

12. Cleaning Cloths and Sponges

13. Steel Scrubbers (for the kitchen)

14. Tupperware-Like Bowls

15. Napkins

. . . ● ● ● ● ● . . .

What does this button do?

Do you ever feel overwhelmed by all the buttons and settings on your home appliances? Whether it's a washing machine, a dishwasher, or an oven, there are so many options and features that it can be intimidating to figure them out. I'm here to show you how to use all those buttons on your home appliances in a fun and easy way. So get ready for a fun journey where we explore each appliance button by button! Let's start with the oven...

How to Use The Oven

1. Start/Stop Button: This button is used to turn the oven on and off.

2. Timer/Clock Button: Used to set an amount of time for your food to cook, or just as a clock if you need one!

3. Temperature Selector Knob: This allows you to adjust the temperature of the oven so that your food can be cooked at a specific temperature (most often measured in degrees Fahrenheit).

4. Bake Control Dial: This dial allows you to choose between baking and broiling options, two different methods of cooking food in an oven by using either

indirect or direct heat sources respectively.

5. Convection Button: When activated, this feature circulates air throughout the oven cavity while cooking, allowing for evenly cooked meals every time!

6. Self-Cleaning Option: This mode uses high temperatures and steam cleaning cycles to remove baked-on grime from inside your oven—no scrubbing necessary!

7. Keep Warm Setting: This setting keeps already cooked dishes warm until serving time without over-cooking them!

8. Preheat Indicator Light/Button: Lights up when preheating is done, letting you know when it's ready.

9. "Bake" and "Broil" are two different ways of cooking food in an oven. "Baking" uses indirect heat, meaning the heat comes from all sides as the oven heats up, while "Broiling" uses direct heat from above or below. Foods that are best cooked using baking include casseroles, cakes, and other dishes that need time to cook slowly. Foods for broiling should be thin cuts of meat or vegetables that need to be cooked quickly on high heat.

How to Use The Dishwasher

1. Detergent Dispenser: This is where you'll add dishwasher detergent, usually in

the form of a tablet or powder.

2. Water Softener Setting: If your water supply has a high level of calcium (also known as hard water), this setting will help reduce it, making it easier to clean dishes and reduce spots.

3. Rinse Aid Dispenser: This setting allows you to add a rinse aid, which will help make dishes look sparkly and spotless after being washed!

4. Cycle Selection Knob: You can choose light wash, normal wash, or heavy duty, depending on how dirty your dishes are.

5. Heated Dry Button: This will activate the heated dry option, which speeds up drying time and makes dishes look even better!

6. Delay Start Option: This allows you to delay when the dishwasher will start running so that you can take advantage of off-peak electricity rates or have your dishes washed in time for dinner.

Tips for properly loading the dishwasher

1. Make sure to load the dishwasher properly, with larger items in the back and small or delicate items on the top rack.

2. Pre-rinsing isn't necessary; modern dishwashers are designed to take care of food debris without needing any extra help from you!

3. Use a specially formulated dishwashing detergent for the best results. This will ensure that your dishes come out spotless every time.

4. Avoid overloading; make sure there is enough space between each item so that water can reach all surfaces of each dish effectively while washing.

5. Utensils should be placed in holders or compartments rather than loose in the bottom of the machine, as they may become damaged during washing cycles if

not secured appropriately.

6. Choose the appropriate settings for your specific load. For example, use a quick wash cycle for lightly soiled dishes or a heavy duty setting for more difficult cleaning tasks like baked-on grease and grime.

How to Do Laundry

1. Type of Fabric Selection Knob: This knob allows you to choose the type of fabric (cotton, synthetic, etc.) that's being washed so that it gets the appropriate cycle and temperature.

2. Water Temperature Knob: You can set this knob to cold or warm depending on the type of fabric being washed and how dirty it is.

3. Spin Speed Selection Knob: Adjust the spin speed to higher or lower, depending on the type of fabric and how delicate it is so that you don't damage your clothes.

4. Delicate Wash Button: Push this button for a gentle cycle that's perfect for delicates like silk, wool, and chiffon.

5. Pre-Soak Button: Use this button to give heavily soiled clothes a pre-soak before the wash cycle starts in order to get rid of tough stains.

6. Extra Rinse Button: This will add an extra rinse cycle to your washing machine,

allowing you to get clothes even cleaner than usual.

7. Timer Knob: Set the timer for how long you want your washer to run so that it can finish before you need to leave home or go to bed!

8. Dry Temperature Selection Dial: This dial enables you to choose between different drying temperatures, depending on the fabric you're drying.

How to Use The Dryer

1. Select the correct temperature setting for the type of fabric you are drying. Generally, low heat is used for delicate items, and high heat is used for heavier fabrics like towels or jeans.

2. Always shake clothes out before putting them in the dryer to ensure that they all dry at an even rate and don't get damaged by being too close together when tumbling around in the drum.

3. Check pockets of garments before placing them into the dryer to avoid any damage that could be caused by metal objects such as keys or coins getting caught up in clothing during a cycle!

4. Avoid overloading your machine with too many items, as this can cause clothes not to tumble freely, which will lead to longer drying times and higher energy bills!

5. Use an appropriate timer setting. Shorter cycles will save energy but might leave damp spots on thicker materials. Longer cycles use more electricity but help prevent shrinkage from excessive heat exposure!

6. Use a cool-down cycle on delicate items like lingerie or wool sweaters so that they won't be damaged by intense temperatures in regular drying cycles!

7. Always empty the lint filter before and after each load to ensure that air can flow freely and that your clothes will dry quickly and efficiently. This also reduces any fire risk due to a build-up of lint in the machine.

Also, clean the lint filter regularly with a brush or a vacuum to get rid of any dust that may have built up.

1. Add a fabric softener sheet to the drum for extra softness and static reduction as well as to give clothes a pleasant scent!

2. Finally, always check each item before taking them out of the dryer to make sure they're not overheated or still damp.

These are some of the important settings and features to consider when working with home appliances but always refer to your appliance manual for more detailed instructions. With these tips in mind, you'll be a master of domestic engineering in no time!

CHAPTER TWO

DON'T STARVE TO DEATH!

G ONE ARE THE DAYS when you had to rely on takeout every day just because you didn't know how to cook! Now, with a little bit of effort and some help from me, you can become your own personal chef. This chapter will teach you everything there is to know about making delicious meals for yourself and your friends, from stocking your pantry to mastering basic cooking techniques to learning the right kitchen equipment. So let's roll up our sleeves, tie on an apron, and start whipping up something amazing! And let's not forget the bonus recipes! After all, what good is a cookbook without delicious recipes to try out? Get ready to make some mouthwatering food that will have everyone asking for seconds. Bon Appetit!

Fun factoid: Before the pandemic, the difference in my mind between cooking and not cooking was simple:

Not cooking = opening a bag of chips

Cooking = putting the chips on a plate with some onion dip

When I was locked in my house like the rest of the world, I discovered that cooking is not only simple but also very relaxing and fun (unless the kitchen is on fire... then it's miles away from relaxing!).

· · · ● · ● · ● · ·

Basic Kitchen Tools and Appliances

First, the basics. What do you need to have in your kitchen?

For someone living alone for the first time, it's important to have the essential tools in your kitchen. Having all the necessities can make cooking and meal preparation much easier and more enjoyable. So let's get started!

For starters, having a good set of pots and pans is essential for any home cook and can make all the difference when it comes to making food quickly and efficiently. In addition, having different types of knives is also important for any home cook. From a chef's knife to a paring knife, having various types of knives can help you with slicing, dicing, and julienning your ingredients. Having the right kitchen equipment and utensils is also essential for making delicious meals. You'll need measuring cups, spoons, and various other tools to get the job done.

Here's a handy list of essentials to help get you started:

- Pots and pans

- Knives (chef knife, paring knife, etc.)

- Measuring cups and spoons

- Cutting board

- Mixing bowls

- Baking dishes/sheets

- Colander or strainer

- Plates and bowls

- Wooden spoon

- Spatula

- Whisk

- Tongs

- Peeler

- Silverware

- Glassware

- Pasta spoon

- Ladle

- Slotted spoon

- Kitchen shears

- Thermometer

- Non-stick skillet

- Saucepan

- Sheet pan

- Immersion blender

- Colander

- Box grater

- Prep bowls

- Cutting board

- Can opener

- Vegetable peeler

- Instant Pot

- Oven mitts and towels

- Paper towel holder

- Toaster oven and/or air fryer

- Well-stocked spice rack

Now, a Decently-Stocked Pantry

Once you've got all the essentials in place, it's time to stock your pantry with delicious ingredients. Having a well-stocked pantry can make all the difference when it comes to meal prepping. From spices and herbs to pasta, rice, and canned goods, having a variety of pantry staples can help you whip up delicious meals in no time!

Here are some basic ingredients you should always have handy so you can whip up any type of meal at a moment's notice:

- Rice

- Tomato sauce

- Baking soda

- Baking powder

- Sugar

- Salt

- Pepper

- Olive oil

- Chicken or vegetable broth

- Condiments (e.g., soy sauce, vinegar)

- Flour

- Spices and herbs (e.g., garlic, oregano)

- Nuts and seeds (e.g., almonds, sunflower seeds)

- Lentils, canned beans (e.g., black beans, chickpeas)

- Grains (e.g., quinoa, bulgur wheat)

- Pasta

- Rice noodles

- Dried fruits

- Coconut milk/cream

- Yogurt/dairy alternative products

- Vegetables and fruits

- Cheese

- Eggs

- Peanut butter and other nut butters

- Tofu

Now, let's dive into the fun stuff—learning to cook! From navigating your way around a kitchen to mastering classic techniques, this section has it all. We'll start off by talking about basic cooking terms and techniques. After that, I'll show you how to meal prep for the whole week so you can save time and energy. And finally, I'll share some delicious recipes so that you can entertain friends and family in style! Let's get this cooking show on the road! Tie on your apron—it's going to be a wild ride!

Mmm, the joys of cooking! The smell of freshly baked bread wafting through your kitchen, the sizzle and pop of a hot pan as you sear meats or veggies—it's enough to make any aspiring chef quiver with excitement. However, before you can create culinary masterpieces in your home, you must first master some fundamentals. From navigating around a kitchen to mastering classic techniques and stocking up on pantry staples, this is everything you need to know about cooking terms and techniques.

· · · ● · ● ● · · ·

Cooking Terms You Should Know

First, let's discuss the different cooking terms and techniques. These are all important skills that every cook should know.

- **Baking**:
  This is a method of cooking food in an oven with dry heat. Cakes, cookies, and bread are all examples of food baked in the oven.

- **Boiling**:
  This is a method of cooking food in boiling water or other liquids like stock. Pasta, potatoes, and vegetables are all examples of things boiled in liquid.

- **Braising**:
  This is a method of slow-cooking by simmering food with a small amount of liquid in a covered pot or pan. Meats and vegetables are often braised to develop a deep, rich flavor.

- **Broiling**:
  This is a method of cooking food in the oven with direct, intense heat from above. Broiling is commonly used to cook steak and other meats, but it's important to watch the food closely as it can burn quickly when broiling.

- **Frying**:
  This is a method of cooking food in hot oil or other fat. Frying is commonly used for foods like French fries, but it's important to use the right type of oil and watch closely when frying, as the food can burn quickly.

- **Grilling**:
  This is a method of cooking over direct heat on a barbecue grill. Meats and vegetables are often grilled to develop an intense smoky flavor.

- **Roasting**:
  This is a method of cooking food in the oven with dry heat from all sides. Commonly used for meats like chicken and turkey, roasting helps seal in the juices and promote even cooking.

- **Sautéing**:
  This is a method of cooking food in a small amount of hot fat or oil. Foods like vegetables and meats are sautéed quickly over high heat to develop flavor.

When cooking, you need to measure the ingredients. This means you need to know how much of each ingredient to add. There are various measurements used when cooking, such as teaspoons, tablespoons, cups, and ounces. You also might see phrases like "pinch" or "dash." Knowing the measurements helps you make sure that your food tastes just right!

Cooking can be a great way to express yourself, but following a recipe is an essential skill for any home cook. Recipes provide guidance and structure that help you craft delicious dishes every time. But when should you stick to the recipe, and when is it safe to deviate from it? Understanding how to read recipes and knowing when it's okay to improvise will take your cooking skills up a notch!

Once you've mastered the basics, why not try meal prepping for the week? Meal prepping helps save time and money by helping you purchase, cook, and store food for the whole week. This way, you can plan out your meals ahead of time and have delicious home-cooked meals on hand throughout the week.

• • • ● • ● • • •

Meal Prepping

Meal prepping is the "adulting" equivalent of doing your taxes. It's not always fun, but it's necessary if you want to eat something other than ramen noodles and cereal for dinner. But, let's be real, who has the time or energy to meal prep for a whole week? That's why I'm here to share some tips and tricks to make meal prep a little less daunting.

First of all, let's talk about recipes. I'm all about keeping things simple, especially when you're living alone for the first time and trying to adult. That's why I recommend picking recipes that have some common ingredients. For example, if you're making a chicken stir-fry one night, you can use the leftover chicken for a salad the next day. Genius, right?

Another tip is to make a big batch of something that you can eat throughout the week. I'm talking about things like chili, soups, or casseroles. These dishes are great because they're easy to make and you can eat them for multiple meals. Plus, they're perfect for those nights when you're too lazy to cook and just want to heat something up.

Now, let's talk about the actual meal preparation process. The key is to make it as easy and painless as possible. That is why I recommend completing all of your preparations in one day. This means chopping vegetables, cooking grains, and marinating meat. Trust me, you'll thank yourself later when you don't have to do all of that work during the week.

Another tip is to invest in some good storage containers. You don't want to spend all of that time meal-prepping, only to have your food go bad because you don't have proper storage. These containers will also make it easier to grab and go when you're in a hurry.

Finally, let's talk about how to make meal prep fun. I know, I know, it sounds impossible, but hear me out. One way to make meal prep more enjoyable is to turn on some music or a podcast. This will help pass the time, and you'll be so focused on the music that you won't even realize you're meal-prepping.

Another way to make meal prep more fun is to make it a social event. Invite a friend over to help you prep, and you can make it a girls' night. Plus, you'll have someone to talk to while you're chopping vegetables.

Meal prep doesn't have to be a daunting task. Just keep things simple, make a big batch of something, and make it a fun event. And remember, if all else fails, there's always ramen and cereal.

Here are some basic recipe ideas to jog your mind whenever you are struggling to come up with something different to eat.

NOTE: The meals marked with an asterisk (*) include an easy-to-follow recipe at the end of the list.

• • • ● • ● • • •

Recipe Ideas:

- Scrambled Eggs
- Macaroni and Cheese*
- Homemade Pizza
- Baked Salmon*
- Roasted Vegetables
- Spaghetti and Meatballs
- Chicken Wings
- Omelette with Veggies

- Quiche Lorraine*

- Avocado Toast

- Peanut Butter and Banana Toast

- Overnight Oats

- Fruit Smoothie Bowls

- Hash Browns with Fried Eggs

- Breakfast Burrito

- French Toast Sticks

- Yogurt Parfait

- Veggie Wraps

- Cobb Salad

- Shrimp Fried Rice*

- Tuna Melt

- Pesto Pasta Salad

- Quesadilla

- Tomato Soup with Grilled Cheese

- Chicken Fajitas*

Mac and Cheese... With a Twist

Mac and cheese is a classic comfort food that can be enjoyed by people of all ages. But why settle for plain old mac and cheese when you can give it a twist? Here's a recipe for "Jalapeño Popper Mac and Cheese" that is sure to please your taste buds:

Ingredients:

- 8 oz. elbow macaroni

- 4 tbsp. butter

- 4 tbsp. flour

- 2 cups milk

- 2 cups shredded cheddar cheese

- 2 jalapeño peppers, diced

- 1/4 cup bread crumbs

- 1/4 cup grated Parmesan cheese

Instructions:

1. Preheat your oven to 350°F.

2. Cook the elbow macaroni according to package instructions. Drain and set aside.

3. In a saucepan, melt the butter over medium heat. Whisk in the flour to form a roux.

4. Slowly pour in the milk while whisking continuously. Cook the mixture until it thickens.

5. Remove the saucepan from heat and stir in the shredded cheddar cheese, diced jalapeño peppers, and cooked elbow macaroni.

6. Pour the mac and cheese mixture into a baking dish.

7. In a small bowl, mix together the bread crumbs and grated Parmesan cheese. Sprinkle the mixture on top of the mac and cheese.

8. Bake in the preheated oven for 25-30 minutes, or until the bread crumb topping is golden brown.

9. Remove from the oven and let it cool for a few minutes before serving.

This recipe gets a nice kick of heat from the jalapeño peppers, which pairs perfectly with the creamy mac and cheese. Enjoy it with a cold beer or a glass of wine and forget the world.

· • ● ●·● ● ● · ·

Baked Salmon

Baked salmon is a healthy and delicious dish that is easy to make at home:

Ingredients:

- 1 lb. salmon fillet

- 2 tbsp. olive oil

- 2 cloves of garlic, minced

- 2 tbsp. lemon juice

- 1 tsp. dried thyme

- Salt and pepper to taste

Instructions:

1. Preheat your oven to 400°F.

2. In a small bowl, mix together the olive oil, minced garlic, lemon juice, thyme, salt, and pepper.

3. Line a baking sheet with parchment paper and place the salmon fillet on it.

4. Brush the olive oil mixture over the salmon, making sure that it is evenly coated.

5. Bake the salmon in the preheated oven for 12-15 minutes, or until it is cooked through and flaky.

6. Remove it from the oven and let it cool for a few minutes before serving.

7. You can serve it with a side of vegetables or a salad, or on top of a bed of rice or quinoa. You could add some sliced lemon on top of the fish for a nice touch. You can also experiment with different herbs and spices to change the flavor profile of the dish. Enjoy!

• • • ● • ● • • •

Quiche Lorraine

Quiche Lorraine is a classic French dish that is perfect for breakfast, lunch, or dinner. It's easy to make and can be tailored to your taste. Here's a simple recipe that a twenty-something-year-old woman with no cooking experience can follow at home:

Ingredients:

- 1 pre-made pie crust (store-bought or homemade)

- 4 slices of bacon, diced

- 1/2 cup diced onion

- 1 cup heavy cream

- 3 eggs

- 1/2 cup grated Gruyere cheese

- Salt and pepper to taste

Instructions:

1. Preheat your oven to 350°F.

2. In a skillet over medium heat, cook the diced bacon until crispy. Remove the bacon from the skillet and place it on a paper towel to drain. Leave the bacon fat in the skillet.

3. Add the diced onion to the bacon fat in the skillet and cook until softened, about 3 minutes. Remove from heat and set aside.

4. In a mixing bowl, whisk together the heavy cream, eggs, grated Gruyere cheese, salt, and pepper.

5. Place the pre-made pie crust in a 9-inch pie dish.

6. Spread the cooked bacon and onions evenly over the bottom of the pie crust.

7. Pour the cream and egg mixture over the bacon and onions.

8. Bake in the preheated oven for 30-35 minutes or until the quiche is set and the top is golden brown.

9. Remove from the oven and let it cool for a few minutes before slicing and serving.

This quiche is perfect for any meal of the day. You can also add other ingredients of your choice, like mushrooms, spinach, or scallions, to make it more exciting. Enjoy!

• • • • • • • • • •

Shrimp Fried Rice

Shrimp fried rice is a delicious and easy dish that is perfect for a quick and satisfying weeknight meal. Here's a recipe for "Shrimp and Vegetable Fried Rice" that you can make at home:

Ingredients:

- 2 cups cooked rice (white or brown)

- 1 lb. shrimp, peeled and deveined

- 1 tbsp. vegetable oil

- 2 eggs, beaten

- 1 onion, diced

- 2 cloves of garlic, minced

- 1 cup frozen peas and carrots

- 2 tbsp. soy sauce

- 1 tbsp. oyster sauce

- Salt and pepper to taste

- Green onions, thinly sliced for garnish

Instructions:

1. In a large skillet or wok, heat the vegetable oil over high heat. Add the beaten eggs and cook, stirring occasionally until they are set and scrambled. Remove the eggs

from the skillet and set them aside.

2. In the same skillet, add the shrimp and cook for 2-3 minutes on each side, or until they are pink and cooked through. Remove the shrimp from the skillet and set aside.

3. In the same skillet, add the onion, garlic, peas, and carrots. Cook for 3-4 minutes, or until they are softened.

4. Add the cooked rice to the skillet and stir to combine with the vegetables.

5. Stir in the soy sauce, oyster sauce, salt, and pepper. Cook for 2-3 minutes, or until the rice is heated through.

6. Add the cooked shrimp and eggs back to the skillet and stir to combine.

7. Garnish with green onions and serve.

You can add other vegetables like diced bell peppers, mushrooms, or bok choy for more variation and color. You can also swap out the shrimp for other proteins like chicken, pork, or tofu. This fried rice is a perfect meal in itself, but if you want to make it fun you can also add diced pineapple for some sweetness.

Chicken Fajitas

Chicken fajitas are a staple in Tex-Mex cuisine and a great option for a quick and easy weeknight dinner. Here's a recipe for "Spicy Chicken Fajitas" that you can make at home:

Ingredients:

- 1 lb. boneless, skinless chicken breasts, sliced into thin strips

- 2 bell peppers (red, green, or yellow), sliced

-

1 onion, sliced

- 2 cloves of garlic, minced

- 2 tbsp. olive oil

- 2 tsp. chili powder

- 1 tsp. ground cumin

- 1 tsp. paprika

- Salt and pepper to taste

- Flour or corn tortillas

Instructions:

1. In a large bowl, mix together the chili powder, cumin, paprika, salt, and pepper. Add the chicken strips and toss to coat evenly.

2. In a large skillet or wok, heat the olive oil over medium-high heat. Add the chicken strips and cook for 4-5 minutes, or until they are browned and cooked through. Remove the chicken from the skillet and set it aside.

3. In the same skillet, add the bell peppers, onions, and garlic. Cook for 3-4 minutes, or until they are softened.

4. Add the cooked chicken back to the skillet and stir to combine with the peppers and onions.

5. Heat the tortillas in a dry skillet over medium heat for about 30-45 seconds on each side, or until they are soft and pliable.

6. Serve the chicken and vegetable mixture on the warm tortillas, and top with your favorite toppings such as guacamole, sour cream, or shredded cheese.

You can also add some diced tomatoes or sliced avocado for some more color and flavor. These fajitas are great as is, but you can also serve them with some salsa or some hot sauce for a little extra heat.

· · · ● · ● · ● · · ·

Healthy Snacking

One of the most important things to keep in mind is making sure you're fueling your body with healthy and nutritious snacks throughout the day.

Healthy snacking doesn't have to be complicated or time-consuming. Here are some easy and delicious snack ideas that you can make at home:

1. **DIY trail mix**: Mix together your favorite nuts, seeds, dried fruit, and a small amount of dark chocolate for a sweet and satisfying snack.

2. **Greek yogurt with berries:** Greek yogurt is a great source of protein, and the berries add a burst of flavor and antioxidants.

3. **Avocado toast:** Spread mashed avocado on whole grain toast and sprinkle with a pinch of salt and pepper for a simple and satisfying snack.

4. **Hard-boiled eggs:** Hard-boiled eggs are a great source of protein and can be made in advance for easy snacking throughout the week.

5. **Roasted chickpeas:** These crunchy little snacks are a great alternative to potato chips. Simply rinse and dry a can of chickpeas; toss with olive oil, salt and your favorite spices; and roast in the oven for 25-30 minutes.

6. **Hummus and veggies:** Pair hummus with raw veggies like carrot sticks, cucumber slices, or bell pepper strips for a satisfying and healthy snack.

7. **Apple slices with almond butter:** Sliced apples with almond butter is a classic combination that is both delicious and nutritious.

8. **Smoothie bowls:** Blend your favorite fruits and veggies with a liquid base like almond milk or yogurt and top with granola, nuts, seeds, and berries for a delicious and healthy snack.

9. **Energy balls:** Roll together a mixture of dates, nuts, seeds, your favorite nut butter, and spices for a quick and easy snack that is perfect for on the go.

10. **Popcorn:** Air-popped popcorn is a whole-grain, low-calorie snack that can be seasoned with herbs and spices for added flavor.

Remember, healthy snacking is all about balance. It's important to listen to your body and eat when you're hungry, but also be mindful of the types of snacks you're choosing. Keep these easy and delicious snack ideas in mind, and you'll be well on your way to a healthy and balanced snacking routine.

Don't be afraid to get creative with your snacks and try new things. If you love experimenting with different flavors, you can also try making your own healthy snacks like homemade granola bars, crackers, or even energy bites. And remember, the key is to prepare your snacks in advance and always have them ready to go so that you don't end up reaching for that bag of chips in the middle of the night!

CHAPTER THREE

GET A SWEET RIDE AND KEEP IT SWEET

Which Car Should You Get?

WHEN IT COMES TO getting your first car, it's important to remember that you're not just buying a hunk of metal; you're buying a ticket to freedom and adventure! (Or, you know, just a way to get to work or school on time.) But seriously, choosing your first car can be a big decision, but don't let it stress you out too much. Here are a few tips to make the process more fun and less overwhelming:

Budget:

Before you even start looking at cars, it's important to figure out how much you can afford to spend. This will help narrow down your options and ensure that you don't get in over your head financially.

Needs vs. wants:

Think about what you'll be using the car for. Will you be mostly driving around town, or will you be taking long road trips? Do you need a car that can fit a lot of groceries, or one that can fit a lot of friends? Knowing your needs will help you make a more informed decision.

Safety:

Safety is a top priority when it comes to cars, especially for young women. Look for cars with high safety ratings and features like airbags and anti-lock brakes.

Reliability:

You don't want to be stranded on the side of the road with a broken-down car. Look for cars with good reliability ratings and a reputation for being dependable.

Test drive:

Once you've narrowed down your options, it's important to test drive the cars you're interested in. This will give you a better sense of how they handle the road and whether or not they're a good fit for you.

Remember, buying a car is a big decision, and it's important to take your time and do your research. With these tips in mind, you'll be well on your way to finding the perfect first car for you.

Don't be afraid to haggle:

Car salespeople expect you to negotiate, so don't be shy about it. Just make sure to do your research and know the fair market value of the car you're interested in before you start talking numbers.

Bring a friend:

Buying a car can be a lot more fun with a friend by your side. Plus, they can give you a second opinion and make sure you're not getting swindled.

Make it a contest:

Turn car shopping into a game by setting a budget and seeing how many cool features you can get within that budget.

Don't be afraid to walk away:

If you don't like the car or the deal, there's no shame in walking away. There are plenty of other fish in the sea (and cars on the lot).

Have fun:

Buying a car should be a fun and exciting experience. Don't let it stress you out too much, and remember to have fun.

• • • • • • • • • •

Leasing vs. Buying

When it comes to getting a car, there are two main options to consider: leasing and buying. Both have their pros and cons, so it's important to understand the differences between them to know which one might be the best choice for you.

Leasing a car can be a great option if you like the idea of driving a new car every few years without having to worry about the long-term commitment of owning a vehicle. With a lease, you'll pay a lower monthly payment than if you were buying the car, and you'll also have the option to trade it in for a newer model when the lease term is up. However, you'll also have to stick to a strict mileage limit, and you'll have to pay extra fees if you go over that limit. Additionally, you'll also be responsible for any damage to the car when the lease is up.

On the other hand, buying a car is a good option if you prefer to own the vehicle outright and have the freedom to drive as much as you want. While the upfront cost of purchasing a car can be higher, you won't have to worry about mileage restrictions or end-of-lease fees for excessive wear and tear. Additionally, you'll have the option to sell the car or trade it in whenever you wish. However, you'll also have to bear the full cost of maintenance and repairs, as well as any long-term depreciation of the vehicle's value.

New vs. Used

There are also two options for buying, which are to buy new or used. Buying a new car can be a great option if you're looking for the latest features and technology as well as the peace of mind that comes with having a brand-new vehicle. However, new cars can be more expensive and will depreciate in value more quickly than used cars. Buying a used car can be a great option if you're looking for a more affordable option. Used cars are more budget-friendly and can be a great value. However, you'll want to be sure to check the car's history and have it inspected by a mechanic before you buy it.

Ultimately, the decision between leasing or buying, or whether to buy new or used, will depend on your personal preferences, budget, and driving needs. Take your time to evaluate the options and consider what's most important to you.

Beware of the Finance Manager

Don't be fooled by the title of "Finance Manager." Yes, I know their title makes it sound like this is a boring person who only deals with numbers and only finalizes the lease agreement, but in reality, they are usually the best salespeople in the dealership. When you're sitting down with the finance manager to finalize your car purchase or lease, they will likely try to sell you a bunch of extra features and services. It can be overwhelming, but don't let them pressure you into buying something you don't need or want. Here are some extras to avoid and some worth considering:

AVOID Extended Warranties:

These can be expensive and often provide coverage that you don't need. Before you buy an extended warranty, you should look over the manufacturer's warranty and make sure you know what it covers.

AVOID Paint and Fabric Protection:

These extras can be costly and may not be worth it. In most cases, regular cleaning and maintenance can keep your car looking new.

AVOID Upgraded Sound Systems:

Unless you're an audiophile, you may not need an upgraded sound system. The standard system that comes with the car is usually more than sufficient.

CONSIDER Maintenance Packages:

These can be worth considering if you want to bundle all your regular maintenance and service into one package. Just make sure to compare the package to the cost of individual services before you buy.

CONSIDER Gap Insurance:

This is worth considering if you're financing your car and you're concerned about owing more on the car than it's worth. Gap insurance will cover the difference if your car is stolen or totaled.

CONSIDER Roadside Assistance:

This can be a worthwhile extra, especially if you're planning on taking a lot of road trips. It can give you peace of mind knowing that help is just a phone call away.

Remember, when you're sitting with the finance manager, don't let them pressure you into buying something you don't need or want. Take your time, do your research, and only add what you think is worth it.

· · · ● · ● · · ·

Protect Your New Car... It's the Law!

Buying car insurance can be overwhelming with all the jargon and different coverage options. Here are a few basic terms you'll want to know before you start shopping for car insurance:

- **Deductible:**

A deductible is the amount of money you pay out of pocket before your insurance kicks in. If you have a $500 deductible and you get into an accident that causes $3,000 in damages, you'll be responsible for paying the first $500, and your insurance will cover the remaining $2,500.

When it comes to deciding on a deductible, it's a bit of a trade-off. A higher deductible will lower your monthly premium, but it also means you'll have to pay more out of pocket if you get into an accident. A lower deductible will increase your monthly premium, but it also means you'll have to pay less out of pocket if you get into an accident.

As a general recommendation for someone who is a first-time car buyer and has limited resources, I would suggest going for a higher deductible. It will lower your premium and help you save on your insurance costs. However, be certain that you are comfortable with the amount you would have to pay out of pocket in the event of an accident. It's always better to have a higher deductible and save a bit of money on the premium, but make sure you have enough savings to cover the deductible if something happens.

If you are someone who is more financially stable and doesn't mind paying a little more, you can opt for a lower deductible. This will give you peace of mind knowing that you won't have to pay as much out of pocket in the event of an accident.

In either case, just make sure you understand your policy and what you're paying for, and always try to shop around and compare different policies and prices from different insurance companies before you make a decision.

- **Liability Coverage:**

This is the minimum coverage required by law in most states. It covers damages or injuries you may cause to another person or their property in an accident that you're found at fault for.

- **Collision Coverage:**

This covers damages to your own vehicle in the event of an accident, regardless of who is at fault.

- **Comprehensive Coverage:**

This covers damages to your vehicle from non-collision incidents such as theft, vandalism, or natural disasters.

- **Uninsured/Underinsured Motorist Coverage:**

This covers damages and injuries to you and your passengers if you're in an accident with someone who doesn't have insurance or doesn't have enough insurance to cover the damages.

How Much Coverage Should You Get?

When it comes to how much insurance you should get, it depends on your age and driving experience. As a young woman in her twenties, you may be able to get away with just the minimum liability coverage required by law, but I would suggest getting more coverage. If you're in an accident, you don't want to be on the hook for thousands of dollars in damages. I would recommend getting a policy that includes liability, collision, and comprehensive coverage.

In terms of dollar amounts, for liability coverage, I would recommend getting at least $100,000 per person/$300,000 per accident for bodily injury liability and $50,000 for property damage liability. For collision and comprehensive coverage, I would recommend getting at least a $500 deductible.

Remember, it's always better to be safe than sorry, so make sure to get enough coverage to protect yourself financially. And don't forget, the more coverage you have, the more peace of mind you'll have on the road. So if you can afford it, go for gold!

• • • ● • ● ● • • •

How to Keep That Sweet Ride, Well... Sweet

Listen up! It's time for you to get the lowdown on basic car maintenance that you should know how to do on your own. And trust me, you don't need to be a genius or have a dad who's a mechanic to do these things. All you need is a little bit of knowledge and a whole lot of determination.

- **Oil Check:**

 First things first, you should know how to check your oil level and change your oil. It's one of the most important things you can do to keep your car running smoothly. And it's not as scary as it sounds, I promise! Just pop the hood, locate the dipstick, pull it out, wipe it off, stick it back in, and pull it out again. The level should be between the two marks on the dipstick. If it's low, add some oil. If it's time for an oil change, go to a professional mechanic or do it yourself.

- **Tire Pressure:**

Next, you should know how to check your tire pressure and rotate your tires. Under-inflated tires can cause all sorts of problems, like poor fuel economy and uneven wear. Make sure you check your tire pressure at least once a month. Inflate the tire to the recommended level located on the sidewall of the tire (also on a sticker on the inside of the driver's door). Rotating your tires will help them wear more evenly and last longer as well.

- **Changing a Flat:**

You should also know how to change a flat tire; it's a basic skill that will come in handy in case of an emergency. Make sure you have a spare tire and a jack in your car, and know how to use them.

Here's a quick, step-by-step guide:

1. First, make sure you are in a safe location away from moving traffic. Turn on your hazard lights to alert other drivers.

2. Locate your spare tire, jack, and lug wrench. These are usually found in the trunk or under the car.

3. Loosen the lug nuts on the flat tire. Do this while the car is still on the ground. It will be harder to loosen them once the car is jacked up.

4. Use the jack to lift the car off the ground. Make sure the jack is securely in place and that the car is stable before proceeding.

5. Remove the lug nuts and flat tire. Carefully place the flat tire to the side.

6. Put the spare tire on the car and replace the lug nuts. Tighten them as much as you can by hand.

7. Lower the car back to the ground.

8. Tighten the lug nuts further with the lug wrench in a crisscross pattern.

9. Put all the equipment back in the trunk.

10. Drive to the nearest repair shop to have your flat tire fixed or replaced as soon as possible.

Remember never to drive on a spare tire at high speed or for a long period of time. A spare tire should only be used to take you to a tire store to get a new one.

- **Check Your Brakes:**

 Another thing you should know is how to check your brakes. If you hear any strange noises or your car pulls to one side when you brake, it's time to get them checked. Always make sure to keep your brake pads in good condition.

Don't Attempt...

 There are some things you should never attempt unless you know what you're doing. For example, if your check engine light is on, don't try to fix it yourself unless you're a pro. It could be something simple like a loose gas cap, but it could also be something serious like a malfunctioning catalytic converter, and if you're not sure what you're doing, you could make things worse.

Never attempt to do any serious electrical work on your car. I've seen some horror stories of people trying to fix their own electrical problems and ending up setting their cars on fire. Trust me, you don't want to go there.

I know that maintaining a car can be intimidating. But with the right knowledge and tools, you can do it! And don't be afraid to ask for help; there's no shame in that.

And, just to keep it fun, here's a true story. I once heard of a friend's wife who took her car to the shop because it was making a strange noise. They took it for a test drive and couldn't figure out what was making the noise. It turned out to be just her phone vibrating inside the glove compartment. She had been getting calls and text messages but didn't realize that the phone was set to vibrate instead of ring. They had a good laugh about it, and she was grateful that it wasn't something serious.

So, always check the obvious before assuming the worst, and maybe keep your phone on ring instead of vibrate when driving!

I have included a Car Maintenance tracker in my free Adulting Hard Workbook. Just visit https://adultinghardbooks.com

CHAPTER FOUR

YOU'RE AN ADULT. FEEL THE PART... LOOK THE PART

W ELCOME TO THIS CHAPTER, where I will be sharing my thoughts and insights on the importance of setting goals, creating a powerful vision, making a bucket list, and road mapping a life plan. I understand that having a clear direction and purpose in life can be challenging, but I believe that with the right mindset and tools, anyone can achieve their goals and live the life they want.

Feel the Part

Setting and achieving goals is a journey that requires consistent effort and determination, but the end results are well worth the effort. With that being said, I am excited to take this journey with you and help you create the life you've always wanted. Let's begin!

But first, let's set the scene with a quote from the great Zig Ziglar:

"A goal properly set is halfway reached."

That's right; by setting specific, measurable, attainable, relevant, and time-bound (SMART) goals, you're already on your way to success. But what about that vision? Well, as author and speaker Tony Robbins says, *"A vision without a plan is just a dream. A plan without a vision is just drudgery."*

So, make sure to not only set those goals but also have a clear vision of where you want to be in the future.

Here are some prompts to help you get started.

1. What is something you've always wanted to learn or try?

2. Where do you see yourself in 5 and 10 years?

3. What is one thing that would make you feel truly accomplished?

4. What is something you've been putting off for too long?

5. What is a dream that you've always had?

6. What is one thing you would change about yourself?

7. What is a skill you would like to master?

8. What is an area of your life that you would like to improve?

9. What is a goal you have for your personal relationships?

10. What is a goal you have for your career?

11. What is a place you've always wanted to visit?

12. What is something you've always wanted to buy?

13. What is a hobby you've always wanted to take up?

14. What is a challenge you would like to overcome?

15. What is a personal record you would like to break?

16. What is a cause you are passionate about and would like to support?

17. What is an event you would like to organize or participate in?

18. What is something you would like to change in your community or society?

19. What is something you would like to achieve for your health and fitness?

20. What is something you would like to achieve for your own personal growth?

SMART goals will provide you with a road map for personal and financial success. Moreover, creating a vision board will keep you motivated every single day.

Vision Board

Having a vision board is a powerful tool that can help you focus on your goals and bring them to life. A vision board is a visual representation of your goals, dreams, and aspirations. It can be a physical board or a digital one, and it is typically filled with images, words, and phrases that represent what you want to achieve in your life.

Creating a powerful vision board starts with setting clear and specific goals. It's important to know exactly what you want to achieve before you start creating your vision board. Once you have your goals in mind, you can start gathering images, quotes, and words that represent those goals. It's important to choose images that evoke strong emotions, as these will be more powerful in helping you achieve your goals.

Another tip for creating a powerful vision board is to make sure that it is in a place where you will see it often. This will help keep your goals at the forefront of your mind and serve as a constant reminder of what you're working towards.

It's also important to regularly review your vision board and make sure it still aligns with your goals and aspirations. If you find that some of the images or words no longer resonate with you, it's okay to change them. A vision board is not a one-time activity but something that should be continuously updated and refined as you grow and change.

Additionally, you can make it interactive by adding things like stickers, post-its, or even a progress tracker. This will not only make it more visually attractive, but it will also help you keep track of your progress and feel a sense of accomplishment as you achieve your goals.

In conclusion, a vision board is a powerful tool that can help you focus on your goals, bring them to life, and make them tangible. Remember to make it specific, place it where you will see it often, review it regularly, and make it interactive. As Jim Rohn said, *"Your life does not get better by chance; it gets better by change."* A vision board can be a powerful tool to change your life and make it better.

Bucket List

Now, onto the bucket list.

"The two most important days in your life are the day you are born and the day you find out why." —Mark Twain

A bucket list is a list of things you want to do in life before you "kick the bucket." The term "bucket list" was popularized by the 2007 film "The Bucket List," starring Jack Nicholson and Morgan Freeman, in which the two main characters make a list of things they want to do before they die.

Creating a bucket list is a great way to set goals for experiences and achievements that will make your life more fulfilling. It's important to have a mix of short-term and long-term goals and to make sure that they align with your values and aspirations.

Here are 20 prompts to help you create a great bucket list:

1. Travel to a specific country or place you've always wanted to visit

2. Learn a new language

3.

Take a cooking class in Italy

4. Go on a safari in Africa

5. Climb a mountain

6. Go scuba diving in the Great Barrier Reef

7. Visit all 7 continents

8. Take a hot air balloon ride

9. Go on a cruise

10. Attend a music festival

11. Try skydiving

12. Go bungee jumping

13. Visit a historical site

14. Go on a road trip

15. Attend a sporting event

16. Go on a camping trip

17. Volunteer for a cause you care about

18. Learn to play an instrument

19. Write a book

20. Take a photography class

It's important to remember that your bucket list is unique to you and should be tailored to your interests and goals. Don't be afraid to think big and dream big; you never know what you can achieve until you try. The goal of a bucket list is to make the most of your life. As Mark Twain said, *"Twenty years from now you will be more disappointed by the things you didn't do than by the ones you did do. So throw off the bowlines. Sail away from the safe harbor. Catch the trade winds in your sails. Explore. Dream. Discover."*

I've included a Bucket Lists sheet as well as a Bullet Journal in the free Adulting Hard Workbook at https://adultinghardbooks.com

• • • • ● • ● • • •

Life Plan

And lastly, a life plan. It's not just about setting goals and making a list; it's about creating a roadmap for the life you want. As the philosopher, Aristotle once said, *"Having a clear and noble purpose in life is the primary and most powerful motivation for living."*

Creating a life plan is an important step in setting and achieving your goals. A life plan helps you focus on what you want to achieve and provides a roadmap for how to get there. Life plans can be broken down into different time frames, such as the next year, the next 5 years, and the next 10 years.

Here are some prompts to help you create a life plan for the next year:

1. Set specific and measurable goals for the 1, 5, and 10 years.

2. Identify the steps you need to take to achieve those goals.

3. Prioritize your goals and determine which ones are most important to you.

4. Create a timeline for achieving your goals.

5. Review your progress regularly and make adjustments as necessary.

So set those goals, build that vision, make that bucket list, and create a life plan that will have you living your best life.

For free templates to help you set goals and create your bucket list, visit https://adultin ghardbooks.com

Breathe.

It's important to remember that setbacks and disappointments are a natural part of the goal-setting process. Sometimes things don't go as planned, and that's okay. The important thing is to not let disappointment discourage you from pursuing your goals.

It's important to set clear and specific goals, but it's also important to be flexible and open to change. Goals may need to be adjusted or even changed altogether as you progress. Don't be afraid to re-evaluate your goals and make changes as needed.

If you're struggling with disappointment, it's important to remember that adjusting your goals is not failure. It's a sign that you're growing and changing, and that's a good thing. It's important to take care of your mental and emotional well-being as well.

In an upcoming chapter, I will be talking about mental health, wellness, and the importance of taking care of yourself as you work towards achieving your goals. I will talk about ways to deal with stress and keep a positive attitude even when things don't go as planned.

Remember, it's not about perfection; it's about progress. Don't be too hard on yourself if you don't reach all of your goals or if it takes longer than you expect to reach them. It's important to celebrate the progress you've made and to keep moving forward. As Helen Keller said, *"Keep your face to the sunshine and you cannot see a shadow."*

• • • ● ● • ● ● • • •

Look the Part

First things first, let's talk about the power of self-confidence. When you look good, you feel good, and that confidence radiates outward, making you even more attractive to others. Now, I know what you might be thinking, "But I'm not a supermodel; how can I ever look good?" And to that, I say, "You don't have to be a supermodel to look like a supermodel. You just have to know how to work with what you've got."

That's where this chapter comes in. We're going to talk about fashion, style, makeup, personal appearance, and maintenance. By the time we're done, you'll have all the tools you need to put your best foot forward and feel like a million bucks. Now, let's get started!

Now, why should you take fashion and style advice from some old guy?

Well you see, just because I'm a man in my 50s, doesn't mean I don't know a thing or two about fashion. In fact, I've been in the fashion industry for over 30 years, working with some of the biggest names in the business. I've been a stylist, a designer, and a fashion editor. I've seen trends come and go, and I've learned what works and what doesn't. Plus, I have an eye for style that's second to none. And let's be real, age ain't nothing but a number, and I'm a forever young spirit who stays on top of the current trends and styles. I may not have the same body as a 20-year-old, but I know how to work with what I have and make it look good. Trust me, I've got this.

Actually, that whole paragraph was completely made up.

I haven't been in the fashion industry or worked with the biggest names in the business. But even though, as a man in my 50s, I may not have the same life experiences and perspectives as a young woman in her 20s, I have a secret weapon. My 22-year-old daughter is a fashion and beauty enthusiast. She keeps me updated on the latest trends and styles, and I have learned a lot from her. I see fashion and style as a way to express oneself and feel confident. That's why my daughter has been a great source of inspiration for me in writing this section. She's always experimenting with new looks and pushing boundaries, and I've been able to learn a lot from her. So, while I may not be a young woman myself, I have a great understanding of what's current and on-trend, thanks to my daughter's influence, and that's what makes me a valuable asset when it comes to giving fashion and style advice.

So buckle up. We both might learn a thing or two!

10 Outfits Every Young Woman Should Have in Her Wardrobe

Creating a versatile wardrobe is key to feeling confident in any situation. You want to have a variety of options that can take you from the office to a night out on the town. Here are some key pieces of advice to consider when building your wardrobe:

1. **A little black dress:** This classic is a must-have for any woman's wardrobe. It's versatile, elegant, and perfect for any occasion.

2. **A tailored blazer:** A nice blazer can dress up any outfit and is perfect for the office or a more formal event.

3. **A pair of comfortable, versatile, and well-fitting jeans:** Every woman should have a good pair of jeans that can be dressed up or down.

4. **A crisp white shirt:** This is a timeless piece that can be paired with anything from jeans to a skirt.

5. **A statement necklace:** Statement necklaces add a touch of glamour to any outfit.

6. **A neutral-colored handbag:** A neutral-colored handbag is a versatile accessory that can be paired with any outfit.

7. **A pair of comfortable and stylish flats:** For those days when you don't want to wear heels.

8. **A pair of neutral-colored pumps:** Every woman should have a pair of classic, neutral-colored pumps in her wardrobe.

9. **A tailored, well-fitting suit:** This can be worn to job interviews, meetings, and formal events.

10. **a casual, comfortable, and stylish outfit:** For casual outings or days off. You

can't be dressed up all the time!

How About Dresses?

Dresses are a great option for any woman looking to build a versatile wardrobe. They're easy to wear and can be dressed up or down depending on the occasion. Here are some key dress styles to consider when building your wardrobe:

A little black dress:
As I mentioned above, this classic is a must-have for any woman's wardrobe. It's versatile, elegant, and perfect for any occasion.

A maxi dress:
Is perfect for summer days or dressy events.

A wrap dress:
Is a versatile option that can be dressed up or down and is suitable for any body type.

A sheath dress:
Is a sleek, elegant option that is perfect for the office or formal events.

A shirt dress:
Is perfect for casual outings or days off.

A cocktail dress:

Is perfect for special occasions, parties, and events.

A sundress:

Is great for summer days, the beach, or outdoor events.

A pencil dress:

Is ideal for the office or formal events.

A midi dress:

Is perfect for any occasion and can be dressed up or down.

An A-line dress:
Is excellent for any occasion and can be dressed up or down.

As with any wardrobe, it's important to invest in quality pieces that are well-made and will last you a long time. And most importantly, always choose pieces that make you feel confident, make you comfortable, and express your personality.

· • • ● • ● • • • ·

If You Spill the Coffee, You Need to Know How to Clean it Up

Listen up, butterfingers, because this is some serious business. Stains happen to the best of us, but that doesn't mean they have to ruin our clothes. Here are some common stains and how to tackle them:

- **Red wine:** This one is a classic party foul. But don't panic! Just pour some white wine on the stain to dilute it, then wash as normal. If you don't have white wine on hand, club soda works too.

- **Grass:** Oh no, you got grass stains at the picnic! Don't worry, just mix some dish soap with water and scrub the stain gently.

- **Chocolate:** We've all been there, sneaking in a snack and getting it all over our clothes. But fear not! Just mix some baking soda and water to make a paste and apply it to the stain. Let it sit for a few minutes, then wash as normal.

- **Coffee:** Crap! You were running late and trying to sip and walk at the same time. Don't freak out; just mix equal parts white vinegar and water and apply it to the stain. Let it sit for a few minutes, then wash as normal.

- **Grease:** You decided to make pancakes in your pajamas and got syrup all over yourself. No problem, just sprinkle some cornstarch on the stain and let it sit for a few minutes, then wash as normal.

- **Blood:** Yikes, you cut yourself cooking and got blood all over your clothes. Don't faint; just soak the stain in cold water for a few minutes, then wash as normal.

- **Makeup:** You were trying to be all fancy with your makeup and ended up getting it all over your clothes. Don't frown, just mix some dish soap and water, then gently scrub the stain.

- **Ketchup:** Oh no, you went a little crazy with the ketchup on your fries. But don't cry; just mix some white vinegar and water, then apply it to the stain. Let it sit for a few minutes, then wash as normal.

As a final piece of advice, always check the care label on your clothes before treating any stains. Some fabrics may be too delicate for certain solutions.

Call Me "Iron Woman"

Now it's time to tackle the dreaded task of ironing. But don't worry, I'm here to make it as painless as possible. Here are some tips and a step-by-step guide on how to iron different garments:

1. Always check the care label on your clothes before ironing. Some fabrics may be too delicate for high heat.

2. Sort your clothes by fabric type and iron them accordingly. For example, cotton can handle higher heat than silk.

3. Lay a press cloth or a dampened towel on top of the garment, which will make ironing more efficient and prevent any shine or burn.

4. Set the right temperature and steam setting for your fabric. For example, silk and nylon should be ironed on a low heat setting, while cotton and linen can handle a higher heat setting.

5. Depending on the item, you usually start at the top and work your way down.

   a. Iron shirts by starting with the collars and cuffs. These areas tend to get the most wrinkled.

   b. Iron pants by starting with the waistband and working your way down to the cuffs. Don't forget to iron the crease on the front of the pants.

   c. Iron skirts by starting with the waistband and working your way down to the hem.

   d. Iron dresses by starting with the collar and working your way down to the hem.

   e. Iron sleeves last since they tend to take the longest.

Once you're done ironing, hang your clothes up immediately to prevent any wrinkles from forming.

Let me tell you a little story. Once upon a time, I decided to iron my shirt while wearing it. It was a hot mess. I ended up with burns all over my shirt and my arms. So, please, just iron your clothes while they're off your body. The end.

So there you have it, ironing simplified (sort of).

Power Tip:

Don't have time or energy to iron your clothes? No problem! Just reach for a wrinkle releaser spray like the one made by Downy. This magical spray will make your clothes look freshly pressed with just a few sprays. Just give your clothes a quick spritz, give them a little shake, and voila! Your clothes will be wrinkle-free and ready to wear. And it's our little secret; don't tell anyone how you achieved that perfectly pressed look without actually having to use an iron.

• • • • ● • ● • • •

Fresh and Fluffy

Finally, this chapter would not be complete if I didn't talk about laundry.

I'm about to give you the ultimate guide to doing laundry like a pro. Let's start with using the washer and dryer.

1. Always check the care label on your clothes before washing them. Some fabrics may be too delicate for the washer and dryer.

2. Sort your clothes by color, fabric type, and soil level. This will help prevent colors from bleeding and ensure that your clothes are washed and dried properly.

3. Use the right amount of detergent for the volume of clothes you're washing. Overusing detergent can leave a residue on your clothes and damage the washer.

4. Use the right water temperature for your clothes. For example, whites and lights can handle hot water, while colors and darks should be washed in cold water.

5. Use the right cycle for your clothes. Delicate fabrics should be washed on a delicate cycle, while heavy-duty fabrics can handle a normal or heavy-duty cycle.

6. Once your clothes are done washing, transfer them to the dryer. Again, sort them

by fabric type and use the right heat setting for each. Delicate fabrics should be dried on a low heat setting, while heavy-duty fabrics can handle a high heat setting.

7. Once your clothes are done drying, remove and fold or hang them promptly to prevent wrinkles and avoid shrinkage of some fabrics.

Going to the Laundromat

Now, let's talk about doing laundry in a public laundromat. It can be a bit overwhelming, but with a little preparation, you'll have clean clothes in no time.

1. Always check the laundromat's hours of operation and machine availability before heading out.

2. Bring your own detergent, fabric softener, and laundry bags. Some laundromats may provide these things, but it's always better to be prepared.

3. Sort your clothes by color, fabric type, and level of soiling. This will help prevent colors from bleeding and ensure that your clothes are washed and dried properly.

4. Pay attention to the machine's instructions and settings. Not all machines are created equal, and you'll want to make sure you're using the right settings for your clothes.

5. Keep an eye on your clothes while they're washing and drying. Laundromats can be busy, and you don't want someone accidentally taking your clothes.

Now you're a laundry pro. Just remember to always check the care label, sort your clothes, and use the right settings for each fabric type. You've got this!

CHAPTER FIVE

HOW WILL YOU PAY FOR EVERYTHING?

L ET'S FACE IT: MONEY can be a scary thing, especially when you're living on your own for the first time. You might be thinking, "I don't have a clue how to manage my finances!" "What if I make a mistake?" "What if I end up penniless and living under a bridge?" But hold your horses! I'm here to tell you that managing your money doesn't have to be scary. In fact, it can be pretty darn fun once you get the hang of it.

Think of it this way: You're about to embark on a wild and exciting adventure, and I'm your trusty sidekick! Together, we'll explore the mysteries of budgeting, taxes, investing, and all the other exciting things that come with being financially responsible. And don't worry, I won't make you sit through boring lectures or use big, complicated words that only Warren Buffett would understand.

We'll keep it light, fun, and (most importantly) easy to understand. So grab a coffee, sit back, and let's take the first step toward financial freedom!

Budget is Not Just a Car Rental Company

Budgeting, my friend, is where the magic happens! It's like putting a GPS on your finances, telling them where to go and what to do. And trust me, you'll want to keep a tight grip on your finances, especially when you're living on your own for the first time.

As the famous business magnate Warren Buffett once said, *"Do not save what is left after spending, but spend what is left after saving."* This quote perfectly illustrates the importance of budgeting. It's all about prioritizing your spending so that you can make sure your money goes where it's most needed.

So let's talk about how to create a budget. It's easier than you might think! All you need is a pen, paper, and a little bit of patience. Start by listing out all of your income, including any part-time work or money you receive from student loans. Then list all of your expenses, including rent, utilities, food, transportation, entertainment, and anything else you can think of.

Now, subtract your expenses from your income. If you're left with a positive number, that's great! You have some extra cash to save or invest. If you're left with a negative number, don't panic. This just means you need to adjust your spending and cut back on some expenses.

For example, instead of eating out for lunch every day, you could pack a sandwich from home. Instead of buying new clothes every month, you could shop at second-hand stores. Little changes like this can add up to big savings over time.

For your convenience, I created some very useful forms that you can download for free at https://adultinghardbooks.com.

That's it! That's the basic process of creating a budget. It might take a little time and effort, but trust me, it's worth it. A budget is like a roadmap to financial stability, and who wouldn't want that?

• • • ● ●• ● ●• ● • • •

Time to Audit Your Financial Situation

A financial audit sounds like a big, scary word, but it's actually a simple process of taking stock of your finances. Just like you'd give your car a tune-up or your body a check-up, a financial audit is a check-up for your money.

The idea behind a financial audit is to identify any areas where you can cut back on spending, find ways to increase your income, and make sure you're on track to meet your financial goals. It's like spring cleaning for your finances!

To do a financial audit, start by gathering all of your financial documents, including bank statements, bills, receipts, and any other records of your income and expenses. Then, take a look at your spending habits and see where your money is going. Are there any expenses that you can cut back on? Are there any areas where you can increase your income?

Next, check your credit report to make sure there are no errors and to see where you stand in terms of your credit score. Make sure you're paying your bills on time and keeping your debt under control.

Finally, take a look at your long-term financial goals, such as saving for retirement, paying off student loans, or buying a home. Make sure you're on track to meet these goals and adjust your budget if necessary.

The key to a successful financial audit is being honest with yourself and making a commitment to change. It's never too late to start taking control of your finances, and a financial audit is a great place to start. So, what are you waiting for? Get auditing!

You can download some handy worksheets for free at https://adultinghardbooks.com.

Your Credit Score

Ah, the mysterious world of credit scores! This three-digit number can be the difference between getting approved for a loan or being stuck with high interest rates. So, let's take a closer look at how it all works.

Your credit score is a number that ranges from 300 to 850 and represents your creditworthiness, or how likely you are to pay back a loan. It's based on information in your credit report, including your payment history, the amount of debt you have, the length of your credit history, and more.

If your score is between 720 and 850, you're considered to have an excellent credit score, and you'll probably get the best loan terms and interest rates. A score between 680 and 719 is considered good, and you'll likely have access to a decent range of loan options. A score between 620 and 679 is considered fair, and you'll likely pay higher interest rates. A score below 620 is considered poor, and you may have trouble getting approved for a loan, or you may get stuck with high interest rates.

To build a good credit score, start by paying your bills on time and keeping your credit card balances low. A long credit history and a mix of different types of credit, such as credit cards, personal loans, and student loans, can also help.

On the flip side, late payments, maxing out your credit cards, and having a lot of new credit applications can negatively impact your credit score.

The benefits of a great credit score are many. For starters, you'll have more loan options available to you, and you'll be able to secure lower interest rates. This means you'll pay less in interest over the life of a loan, and you'll have more money in your pocket each month.

A good credit score can also open doors for you in other areas of your life, such as getting approved for an apartment or getting a better insurance rate.

How do I Get My Credit Report?

Now that you know the importance of your credit score, you may be wondering where you can find it. Well, there are a few different ways to get a glimpse of your credit score:

- **Free credit report:**

By law, you are entitled to one free credit report per year from each of the three major credit bureaus: Experian, Equifax, and TransUnion. You can request your reports at AnnualCreditReport.com. It's important to note that this is not your actual credit score, but it will give you a good idea of the information that's being used to calculate your score.

- **Credit card issuers:**

Some credit card issuers, such as Discover and Capital One, offer free credit scores to their customers. Check with your issuer to see if this is an option for you.

- **Credit score websites:**

There are a number of websites that offer free credit scores, such as Credit Karma and NerdWallet. Just be aware that these scores may not be the same as the ones used by lenders.

When you receive your credit report, it's important to take a close look at the information that's included. Your credit report will include information about your credit accounts, such as credit cards and loans, as well as your payment history, outstanding debt, and more. If you spot any errors or inaccuracies, it's important to dispute them right away, as they could be hurting your credit score.

Checking your credit score is a great way to stay on top of your financial health. Whether you request a free credit report or use a credit score website, it's important to know what information is being used to calculate your score and to take steps to improve it if necessary. By doing so, you'll be on your way to building a strong financial future!

· · · · **·** · **·** · · ·

Death and Taxes

Well... just taxes.

Alright, let's get down to the nitty-gritty. I'll give it to you straight: taxes can be a real headache. But don't panic! I'm here to help you navigate the maze of taxes and come out on the other side with a smile on your face—and hopefully some money in your pocket!

I want to make it clear that I am not giving you professional tax advice. Tax laws are complex and constantly changing, so it's always a good idea to consult a tax professional if you have questions or concerns. With that being said, let's talk about how a young woman should start thinking about taxes.

First things first, let's talk about why taxes are so important. As the famous businessman and philanthropist Warren Buffett once said, *"Only when the tide goes out do you discover who's been swimming naked."* In other words, taxes can be a real eye-opener about your financial situation. By understanding your taxes, you'll be able to see exactly where your money is going and make informed decisions about your financial future.

Now, let's talk about how taxes work. The government collects taxes in a variety of ways, including federal income tax, state income tax, sales tax, and more. It can be overwhelming, but don't worry—there are ways to minimize the amount of taxes you owe. One of the best ways to do this is by taking advantage of deductions. A deduction is a sum that can be taken off of your taxable income, which lowers the amount of taxes you have to pay. Some common deductions include charitable contributions, mortgage interest, and state and local taxes.

When it comes to doing your taxes, you have a few options. If you have a simple tax situation, such as only having a W-2 form and a few deductions, you may be able to do your taxes yourself using tax software like TurboTax or H&R Block. These programs can be a great option for young women just starting out, as they are affordable (generally ranging from $0 to $150) and user-friendly.

However, if your tax situation is more complex, it may be in your best interest to use a tax professional. Tax professionals can range in price from $150 to $500 or more, depending on the complexity of your tax situation. A tax professional can help you understand the complicated tax code and make sure you use all the deductions and credits that you are eligible for.

It's important to note that taxes are normally due on April 15th each year, but if you're not ready to file by then, you can request an extension. Just keep in mind that an extension is only for filing your taxes, not for paying them.

In short, taxes can be a real headache, but by understanding the different ways the government collects tax money and taking advantage of deductions, you can minimize the amount you owe. And whether you decide to do your taxes yourself or use a professional, just remember that taxes are an important part of your financial journey. So, take a deep breath and dive in—I have faith in you!

· · · ● · ● · ● · · ·

Make Your Money Work For You

Investing money can be a confusing task, but it's one of the most important steps to building wealth over time. Here's my take on the subject:

You see, there are two types of interest: simple and compound. Simple interest is like getting a participation trophy. You get a little bit of money just for showing up. On the other hand, compound interest is like being a superhero. Your money starts working for you day and night, even when you're sleeping.

Simple interest is just that: simple. It's calculated solely on the initial principal, or amount of money invested. Let's say you invest $100 and earn 5% simple interest. After one year, your investment will have grown to $105.

Compound interest, on the other hand, is a little more complex (pun intended). It takes into account both the initial principal and the interest that has been added over time. This means that the interest earned in one period becomes part of the principal for the next period, so your investment grows at an exponential rate. For example, let's say you invest $1,000 and earn 5% compound interest, compounded annually. After one year, your investment will have grown to $1,050.00. After two years, it will have grown to $1,102.50. After ten years, it will have grown to $1,628.89! You can see how quickly compound interest can add up over time!

So if you want to really make your money work for you, it's a good idea to focus on invest-ments that compound your interest. As Albert Einstein once said, *"Compound interest is the eighth wonder of the world. He who understands it earns it...he who doesn't...pays it."*

Now, when it comes to investing, there are a ton of options out there. You've got stocks, bonds, mutual funds, real estate, you name it. It can be overwhelming, I know. I've got you covered.

First, let's talk about stocks.

 Stocks are a type of investment that gives you partial ownership of a company. When a company does well, the value of its stock typically increases, and you can sell your stock, hopefully for a profit. When a company does poorly, its stock value may decrease.

To understand stocks better, think of a pie. Each stock is a slice of that pie. When the company does well, the pie gets bigger, and your slice of the pie is worth more. When the company does poorly, the pie may shrink, and your slice of the pie is worth less.

There are two main strategies when it comes to investing in stocks: **growth investing and value investing**. Growth investing involves buying stocks in companies that are growing rapidly and have a lot of potential for future growth. Value investing is buying stocks in companies that are undervalued but have solid fundamentals and the potential for long-term growth.

It's important to do your research before investing in stocks. Look at a company's financial statements, management team, and competition. A company's history of paying divi-dends (a portion of the company's profits paid to shareholders) is also a good indicator of its financial stability.

As the famous investor Peter Lynch once said, *"In this business, if you're good, you're right six times out of ten. You're never going to be right nine times out of ten."* Investing in stocks is a long-term game and requires patience and discipline.

Investing in stocks can feel overwhelming in the beginning, but it doesn't have to be. Here are a few tips to help you get started:

- **Diversification**:

Don't put all your eggs in one basket. Diversification is key when it comes to investing in stocks. Spread your investments across different industries, market caps, and even geographical locations to reduce the risk of losing all of your money if one sector or company performs poorly.

- **Do Your Research:**

Make sure you understand the companies you are investing in. Research the company's financials, management, and industry. The more you know about the company, the better decisions you can make.

- **Start Small:**

Don't try to make a fortune overnight. Start with a small amount of money and add more as you feel more comfortable and learn more about the stock market.

- **Fees:**

Be aware of the fees you'll pay when investing in stocks, such as brokerage fees, management fees, and trading fees. These fees can add up and eat into your returns, so it's important to choose a brokerage with low fees.

- **Time is Your Friend:**

Remember that investing in stocks is a long-term game. The stock market can be volatile in the short-term, but over the long-term, it has historically yielded returns that beat inflation. So if you're in it for the long haul, try not to get too caught up in short-term fluctuations.

"The four most dangerous words in investing are: 'This time it's different.'"
- Sir John Templeton, investor and philanthropist.

I'm Bond... Just Bond

Next, we've got bonds. You can think of them as a loan to a company or the government. They pay you interest over time, and then you get your original investment back at the end. Bonds are a bit more stable than stocks, but they also generally offer lower returns than stocks.When it comes to bonds, the goal is to lend money to an organization or government in exchange for interest payments over a set period of time. When you invest in bonds, you are essentially becoming a lender. Bonds are seen as a less risky investment than stocks because you are sure to get regular interest payments. However, it's important to note that the price of bonds can fluctuate, which can impact the overall return on your investment.

Here are some tips to keep in mind when investing in bonds:

- **Diversification:**

As with any investment, it's important to diversify your portfolio. This means investing in a variety of bonds with different maturity dates and issuers.

- **Credit rating:**

Before investing in a bond, check the credit rating of the issuer. Bonds with a high credit rating have a much lower risk of default but also have lower returns.

- **Maturity date:**

Consider the maturity date when investing in bonds. Long-term bonds tend to offer higher returns, but they also come with more risk. Short-term bonds are generally less risky but offer lower returns.

- **Fees:**

When you buy bonds, you may have to pay fees like transaction fees and management fees. These fees can eat into your returns, so it's important to be aware of them.

In the words of Benjamin Franklin, *"An investment in knowledge pays the best interest."* By taking the time to learn about bonds and other types of investments, you can make sure that your future finances are safe.

Mutual Funds and ETFs

Mutual funds and ETFs are two of the most popular investment options. Both are a mix of stocks and bonds, managed by a professional. They're great options for someone who wants to diversify their portfolio, but they often come with higher fees. A mutual fund is a type of investment vehicle that pools money from multiple investors to buy a diverse mix of stocks, bonds, or other securities. This means that you are pooling your money with other investors to buy a portfolio of assets managed by a professional fund manager. Putting money into a mutual fund is a good idea because it gives you instant diversification, which helps lower your risk.

ETFs, or Exchange-Traded Funds, work similarly to mutual funds in that they pool money from multiple investors to buy a diversified portfolio of assets. The difference is that ETFs are traded on stock exchanges, just like individual stocks. This allows for more flexibility and potentially lower fees compared to mutual funds.

Real Estate

Finally, there's real estate.

First of all, it's important to know that real estate can be a great way to build wealth, and you don't necessarily need a lot of money upfront to get started. There are several ways to invest in real estate, such as through rental properties, real estate investment trusts (REITs), and even crowdfunding.

For young people just starting out, a good strategy is to invest in a rental property. This will allow you to earn passive income in the form of rent, which can help offset the costs of the property. You could also look into REITs, which allow you to invest in real estate without having to buy or manage a property yourself.

The benefits of investing in real estate are numerous. Real estate is a tangible asset, which means it has real value and can appreciate over time. Rental properties can also be a source of passive income, and REITs can give you a steady stream of dividends.

Investing in real estate can be a great way to build wealth, and there are several options available to young people with limited funds. Just remember, as with any investment, it's important to do your research and understand the risks involved.

But here's the thing: the earlier you start investing, the better. Remember that quote from Albert Einstein I mentioned above? Compound interest is your friend, so don't wait; start investing now and watch your money grow over time.

And if you're looking for a change from Warren Buffett, how about this quote from the legendary investor, Peter Lynch? *"If you spend more than 13 minutes analyzing economic and market forecasts, you've wasted 10 minutes."* So don't get too caught up in the details; just start investing and let the magic of compound interest work its wonders for you.

There are many resources available both online and offline that can help you become a better investor. Some popular online resources include financial news websites like Forbes, Wall Street Journal, and CNBC; financial education websites like Investopedia and NerdWallet; and online forums and discussion boards where you can connect with other investors. You can also find financial advisors, wealth management services, investment planning tools, and calculators online. In person, you can attend financial seminars, workshops, and classes, and you can work with a financial advisor to develop an investment plan tailored to your individual needs. Public libraries often have a wealth of financial planning books and resources that are available for free.

· · · ● ●· ● ● · ·

Save Yourself!

When it comes to saving money, there are a few popular strategies you can use to allocate your hard-earned cash. Here's the lowdown on each one:

- **Emergency fund:**

An emergency fund is a savings account set aside specifically for unexpected expenses, like a car repair or a medical bill. It's recommended to save up 3-6 months worth of living expenses in this fund. As the wise man Benjamin Franklin once said, "An ounce of prevention is worth a pound of cure."

- **High-yield savings account:**

A high-yield savings account pays a higher interest rate than a traditional savings account. It's a great option for keeping your savings safe, and it grows over time.

- **Investment account:**

An investment account, like a brokerage account, allows you to invest in stocks, bonds, and other securities. This is a great option for long-term savings goals, like a down payment on a home or retirement.

- **Certificate of Deposit (CD):**

A CD is a savings product that pays a fixed interest rate for a set period of time, typically ranging from 3 months to 5 years. It's a great option for people who want a guaranteed return on their savings.

- **The 50-30-20 Method:**

With this method, you allocate 50% of your income to necessities, 30% to wants, and 20% to savings and debt repayment.

For example, let's say you earn $2,000 a month after taxes. Using the 50-30-20 method, $1,000 should go toward necessities like rent, groceries, and bills. $600 can go toward wants, such as entertainment and eating out, and $400 should go toward savings and debt repayment.

- **The 60-40 Method:**

Using this method, you allocate 60% of your income to necessities and wants, and the remaining 40% goes to savings and debt repayment.

For example, if you earned $2,000 a month, then $1,200 would go towards necessities and wants, and $800 would go towards savings and debt repayment.

- **The Zero-Based Method:**

Under this method, you allocate every dollar you earn to a specific category and have a zero balance at the end of the month.

For example, if you earned $2,000 a month, you could allocate $1,000 towards necessities, $600 towards wants, $200 towards savings, and $200 towards debt repayment. This way, you've accounted for every single dollar you've earned.

- **The Envelope System:**

This strategy involves dividing your spending money into categories, such as groceries, entertainment, and transportation, and then putting cash into different envelopes for each category. Having a physical representation of your budget can help you stay on track for your financial goals.

- **Pay Yourself First:**

This strategy, also known as reverse budgeting, involves setting aside a portion of your income each month to go directly into savings before you pay any bills or make any purchases. Base the rest of your spending on what's left after saving.

- **The 72-Hour Rule:**

This strategy involves waiting 72 hours before making a big purchase to give yourself time to think it over and determine whether it's a necessary expense.

- **The 30-Day Challenge:**

This strategy involves saving a set amount of money each day for 30 days, gradually building up your savings over time.

These are popular strategies to help allocate your savings and make the most of your income. The key is to find a method that works for you and stick to it. Remember, consistency is key!

• • • ● • ● • • •

Slash Those Expenses!

Okay, let's talk about cutting expenses.

First of all, let's do a subscription audit. This is where you go through all your monthly expenses and see if you're actually using all the services you're paying for. You'll be surprised at how many forgotten apps you'll find hiding in there!

Now, let's negotiate. Yes, negotiate! This is where you call up the companies you're paying for and ask for a better deal. Think of it like haggling at a market, but with a telephone instead of a crowded street. Don't be afraid to ask for a discount or to see if they have any promotions going on. And remember, the worst they can say is no.

Here are some tips on how to negotiate:

- Know your stuff. Before you call, do your research. Know how much the same service costs with other companies and be prepared to use that information.

- Be friendly but firm. The customer service rep is more likely to help you if they feel like you're a nice person.

- Don't be afraid to threaten to cancel. Sometimes companies will give you a better deal if they know you're considering leaving.

- Timing is everything. Try to call at the end of the month or quarter when companies are trying to meet their sales goals.

- Remember, it never hurts to ask. So get on the phone and start negotiating like a pro!

Making a Big Purchase

Making big purchases can be exciting, but it's also important to make smart financial decisions. To ensure you get the best value for your money, it's important to know the best circumstances for buying certain items. Here are a few tips:

- **Timing is key:**

Some items go on sale at specific times of the year. For example, winter clothing is often discounted in early spring, while summer clothing is often discounted in late summer or early fall. Furniture and mattresses are often discounted around Memorial Day and Labor Day.

- **Do your research:**

Compare prices and look for sales and discounts before making a big purchase. Consider using price comparison websites or apps to find the best deals.

- **Financing:**

If you need to finance a purchase, consider using a low-interest credit card or taking out a personal loan. It's important to understand the terms and interest rates of any loan or credit card before signing up.

- **Big items:**

When it comes to big items like a car or a home, it's important to do your research and compare prices. Keep in mind that financing options can vary greatly, and it's important to understand the terms and interest rates.

- **Travel**:

Timing is key when it comes to travel. Consider booking flights either in advance or last minute to find the best deals. Consider traveling during the off-peak season to get the best value for your money.

- *Airline tickets:*

Airline ticket prices can vary greatly depending on the time of year and day of the week. Consider booking tickets either in advance or last minute to find the best deals.

"The best time to buy anything is when it's on sale." —Suze Orman

"My favorite two brands are Sale and Clearance." —Jeffrey Chapman
(yes, that's my quote)

• • • ●•● • •• •

When All Else Fails, Earn More Money

You can only cut expenses and save money up to a point. After that, you need to increase the amount of money that comes in.

"The future belongs to those who prepare for it today." —Malcolm X

Getting ready for a job search requires preparation and self-reflection. Here are some steps to help you get started:

- **Assess your skills and experience:**

Make a list of your strengths, areas for improvement, and the skills you've acquired through previous jobs and education.

- **Research potential employers and industries:**

Look for companies that align with your values and goals, and study their mission, culture, and job openings.

Update your resume and cover letter:

- **Resume:**

Tailor it to the specific job you're applying for and highlight your relevant skills and achievements. Use keywords found in the job description and keep it concise and easy to read.

Cover letter:

Show enthusiasm for the job and explain why you're the best fit for the role. Mention specific skills and experiences that make you a good match for the company and position.

Optimize your LinkedIn profile:

Upload a professional headshot and profile summary that showcases your skills and experience.

Connect with people in your desired industry and actively engage with relevant posts. Use LinkedIn to network and research companies and consider adding relevant volunteer work, certifications, and publications to your profile.

Make a job search plan:

Set achievable goals and track your progress. Make a list of the companies and positions you want to apply for and schedule time each day or week to focus on your job search.

"Success is not final, failure is not fatal: it is the courage to continue that counts." —Winston Churchill. Keep pushing forward and don't be discouraged if you don't get a job right away. Keep learning and growing and remember that the job search process is an opportunity for personal and professional development.

What Should You Look For in a Job?

"Equality is not just about sharing opportunities; it's about creating them."
—Melinda Gates

Workplace equality is a crucial aspect of a healthy and fair work environment. Here are some things to look for when evaluating a potential employer's commitment to equality:

Diversity and inclusion policies:

Look for companies that have a clear commitment to diversity and inclusion and have policies in place to support it. This may include initiatives aimed at hiring and promoting a diverse workforce as well as creating an inclusive workplace culture.

- **Equitable pay and benefits:**

Ensure that the company provides equitable pay and benefits to all employees, regardless of gender, race, sexual orientation, etc.

- **Non-discrimination policies:**

Make sure that the company has a clear non-discrimination policy and that employees are protected from harassment and discrimination.

- **Flexible work arrangements:**

Look for companies that offer flexible work arrangements, such as remote work or flexible hours, which can help promote equity for employees with different needs and responsibilities.

- **Employee feedback and involvement:**

Evaluate how the company listens to and involves its employees in decision-making and how it responds to feedback and concerns.

Remember, workplace equality is not only the right thing to do, but it also benefits the company by creating a more engaged and productive workforce. *"Diversity is not about how we differ. Diversity is about embracing one another's uniqueness."* —Ola Joseph

You Don't Get What You Deserve, You Get What You Negotiate

"Don't be afraid to ask for what you want. The worst that can happen is someone will say no." —Richard Branson

Negotiating a salary or raise can be nerve-wracking, but it's an important part of achieving financial stability and career growth. Here are some tips to help you prepare:

- **Research market rates:**

Look at salary surveys and online resources to determine the average pay range for your position and industry. This information will give you a starting point for negotiating your salary.

- **Know your worth:**

Consider your skills, experience, and accomplishments and be prepared to articulate why you deserve a raise or higher salary.

- **Be confident:**

Believe in your value and approach the negotiation with a positive and confident attitude.

- **Ask for what you want:**

When negotiating, be clear and specific about what you want. If you're negotiating a salary, state your desired salary range. If you're negotiating a raise, state the amount you're asking for.

- **Consider non-monetary benefits:**

If a higher salary is not possible, consider asking for non-monetary benefits such as more flexible work hours, more vacation time, professional development opportunities, etc.

- **Be prepared to compromise:**

Be open to compromise and be willing to consider alternatives that meet both your and your employer's needs.

Remember, negotiating a salary or raise is a process and requires patience and persistence. Keep in mind that *"Successful negotiations require preparation, communication, and the ability to compromise."* —John C. Maxwell

CHAPTER SIX

LOOK OUT!

B EING A SINGLE YOUNG woman living on your own can be a thrilling experience, but it's important to be aware of the potential dangers that may come your way. From online scams to unexpected emergencies, it's always wise to be prepared. With that in mind, let's explore the different ways to stay safe, both online and offline, and how to handle different situations if they arise. It's all about being proactive and knowing what steps to take to protect yourself.

Online Safety

 It is just as important to be safe online as it is offline! Because so much of our sensitive personal information is stored and shared online, it's important to be aware of common cybersecurity scams. Here are some of the most common ones to look out for:

- **Phishing scams:**

These are emails or messages that look like they're from a reputable source, but in reality, they're from scammers trying to steal your personal information. They often ask you to click on a link and enter your login credentials, social security number, or other sensitive information. Beware of emails that ask for personal information, no matter how legitimate they look.

- **Fake giveaways and promotions:**

Have you ever received an email claiming you've won a prize or a contest you don't remember entering? It's probably a scam. The scammers will ask you to provide your personal information or to send money to claim your "prize".

- **Malware attacks:**

These are viruses or other malicious software that can infect your device and steal your personal information. Always keep your security software up to date and be cautious when downloading attachments or visiting unknown websites.

To avoid falling for these cyber-scams, here are a few tips:

- Don't click on links from unknown or suspicious sources.

- Verify the source before entering any personal information.

- Keep your security software up to date.

- Don't believe everything you see online, even if it looks legitimate.

And remember, if something seems too good to be true, it probably is! Stay safe online and always trust your gut instinct.

• • • ● • ● • • •

Safe at Home

Staying safe at home is just as important as staying safe online or on the streets. There are a number of emergencies that can happen in the home, from fires to break-ins to medical emergencies. It's important to be prepared for these types of situations so that you can respond quickly and effectively. Here are a few tips to stay safe:

- Install smoke detectors and test them regularly.

- Make sure all doors and windows are securely locked.

- Keep emergency numbers handy, such as the fire department and local hospital.

- Consider getting a home security system to deter intruders.

- Have an evacuation plan in case of a fire or other emergency.

- Keep a basic first aid kit in the house.

By taking these simple steps, you can keep yourself and your home safe in the event of an emergency. Remember, it's always better to be prepared than to be caught off guard.

• • • ● • ● • • •

Only You Can Prevent a House Fire

According to the National Fire Protection Association (NFPA), cooking equipment is the leading cause of home fires and home fire injuries in the U.S[1]. In 2019, nearly half of all home fires started in the kitchen. Working smoke detectors can greatly increase the chances of survival in the event of a fire; the NFPA reports that having working smoke

---

1. National Fire Protection Association (NFPA). (n.d.). Cooking. Retrieved from ht tps://www.nfpa.org/Public-Education/By-topic/Top-causes-of-fire/Cooking.

detectors can reduce death by fire by half. So make sure to follow these tips to keep your home as safe as possible!

1. Keep flammable materials away from heat sources like stoves and heating elements.

2. Don't leave cooking food unattended on the stove.

3. Don't overload electrical outlets and make sure to use proper wiring and light bulbs.

4. Keep curtains, towels, and other flammable materials away from light fixtures.

5. Don't smoke in bed.

6. Have working smoke detectors on every level of your home and in every bedroom.

7. Test smoke detectors monthly and replace the batteries annually.

8. Have a fire escape plan and practice it with your family.

9. Store flammable liquids like gasoline and propane outside of your home.

10. Keep fire extinguishers easily accessible and know how to use them.

How to Use a Fire Extinguisher

There are several types of fire extinguishers, each designed for specific types of fires:

1. Class A: For ordinary combustibles such as wood, paper, and cloth.

2. Class B: For flammable liquids and gases such as gasoline, oil, and natural gas.

3. Class C: For electrical fires caused by appliances, wiring, and other electrical equipment.

4. Class D: For fires involving flammable metals like magnesium, titanium, and potassium.

5. Class K: For kitchen fires involving cooking oils and fats.

When using a fire extinguisher, it's important to remember the acronym PASS: Pull, Aim, Squeeze, and Sweep.

1. Pull the safety pin at the top of the extinguisher to break the tamper seal.

2. Aim the nozzle at the base of the fire, not at the flames.

3. Squeeze the handle to release the extinguishing agent.

4. Sweep the nozzle back and forth across the base of the fire.

Fire extinguishers range in price from around $20 to $200, depending on the type, size, and features. You can buy fire extinguishers at hardware stores, home improvement stores, and online retailers.

It's important to use the right type of fire extinguisher for the specific type of fire you're dealing with. For example, using water on a grease fire in a kitchen can cause the fire to spread, and using a Class A extinguisher on an electrical fire can be ineffective and potentially dangerous. If you're not sure what type of fire you're dealing with, it's always best to evacuate the building and call the fire department.

Stay Dry... Especially Inside!

Home flooding caused by heavy rain, melting snow, broken pipes, or other factors can be a common problem for renters. According to the National Flood Insurance Program, just one inch of water in a home can cause over $25,000 in damages[2], and renters often don't have insurance to cover the costs.

To mitigate damage from home floods as a renter, consider the following tips:

1. Notify your landlord if you notice any water damage or leaks.

---

2. National Flood Insurance Program (NFIP). (n.d.). The cost of flooding. Retrieved from https://www.floodsmart.gov/cost-flooding.

2. Store important documents and valuables in waterproof containers.

3. Be mindful of the weather forecast and take precautions if necessary.

4. Consider purchasing renter's insurance that covers flood damage.

If a flood occurs in your rented home, it's important to take immediate action.

1. Notify your landlord as soon as possible.

2. Move your furniture and valuables to higher ground.

3. Document the damage and take photos for your records.

4. Hire a professional water damage restoration company if necessary or ask your landlord to handle it.

It's also important to evacuate your home if there's a risk of flash flooding or if you're advised to do so by local authorities. Your safety should be your top priority.

A Whole Lotta Shaking Going On

Earthquakes, hurricanes, and tornadoes are all natural disasters that can cause serious damage and threaten lives. Here's a brief overview of how each is measured and what you can do to stay safe:

- **Earthquakes:**

The Richter scale is used to measure earthquakes. It measures the size of the seismic waves that the earthquake makes. The higher the number, the more intense the earthquake.

Here are some tips on how to stay safe during an earthquake:

1. Drop, cover, and hold on: Drop to the ground, take cover under a sturdy piece of furniture, and hold onto it to protect yourself from falling objects.

2. Evacuate if you're in a high-rise building: High-rise buildings are more vulnerable to earthquakes, so it's important to evacuate if you're in one.

3. Stay away from windows: Windows can shatter during an earthquake, so it's important to stay away from them.

4. Know where gas shut-off valves and electrical panels are: In case of gas leaks or electrical hazards, it's important to know how to turn off the gas and electricity in your home.

5. Have a disaster kit on hand: A disaster kit should include food, water, a first-aid kit, a flashlight, and other essentials.

6. Plan and practice an evacuation route: Have a plan in place for how you'll evacuate your home if necessary, and practice it so that you're prepared if an earthquake occurs.

7. Be prepared for aftershocks: Earthquakes are often followed by aftershocks, which can be just as dangerous as the initial earthquake. Stay vigilant and continue to follow safety protocols even after the main event.

Remember that the most important thing to do during an earthquake is protect yourself and act quickly to limit the risk to your safety. Stay informed and listen to what the local government tells you to do to stay safe during and after an earthquake.

- **Hurricanes:**

Hurricanes are measured using the Saffir-Simpson scale, which classifies the storm based on its wind speed and potential for damage. The higher the number, the more intense the storm.

Here are some tips on how to stay safe during a hurricane:

1. Evacuate if told to do so: If local authorities issue an evacuation order, it's important to follow the order and evacuate as soon as possible.

2. Prepare your home: Before the hurricane hits, secure loose outdoor objects, cover windows with shutters or tape and store important documents in a safe and easily accessible place.

3. Stock up on supplies: Make sure you have enough food, water, and other essen-

tials to last for several days without power.

4. Practice your evacuation route: Plan and practice an evacuation route in case you need to leave your home quickly.

5. Stay informed: Stay informed about the latest developments and advice from local authorities through official channels such as the National Hurricane Center and local news outlets.

6. Avoid flood waters: Flood waters can be contaminated and dangerous, so it's important to avoid them.

7. Stay away from windows: High winds can break windows and cause damage, so it's important to stay away from windows during a hurricane.

- **Tornadoes:**

The Enhanced Fujita scale is used to classify tornadoes based on how fast their winds are and how much damage they could do. The higher the number, the more intense the tornado.

Here are some tips on how to stay safe during a tornado:

1. Know the warning signs: Familiarize yourself with the warning signs of a tornado, including a loud roar, a green or yellow sky, and large hail.

2. Take cover: If a tornado is approaching, take cover in a low-lying area, such as a basement or an interior room on the lowest floor of a building. Avoid windows and protect yourself with something sturdy, such as a mattress or a cushion.

3. Make a plan: Make a plan with your family and practice it so that everyone knows what to do in case of a tornado.

4. Stay informed: Stay informed about the latest developments and advice from local authorities through official channels such as the National Weather Service and local news outlets.

5. Avoid mobile homes: Mobile homes are not safe during tornadoes, so seek

shelter in a nearby building if you live in one.

6. Avoid driving: Do not try to drive during a tornado, as it's difficult to see, and it's dangerous to be on the road.

7. Be prepared for after the storm: After the tornado, be prepared for power outages, road closures, and other challenges. Have a plan for communicating with your family and accessing basic necessities.

• • • ●• ● • • •

Personal Safety

Self-defense is an important aspect of personal safety for single women. Here are some sobering statistics in the US:

Physical Violence:

1. The National Domestic Violence Hotline states that 1 in 3 women in the US have experienced physical violence by an intimate partner[3].

2. The National Institute of Justice reported that in 2017, nearly 2 million women in the US were physically assaulted by an intimate partner[4].

---

3. National Domestic Violence Hotline. (n.d.). Domestic Violence Statistics. Retrieved from .

4. National Institute of Justice. (November 9, 2017). Sexual Assault Cases: Exploring the Importance of Non-DNA Forensic Evidence. Retrieved from https://nij.ojp.gov/topics/articles/sexual-assault-cases-exploring-importance-non-dna-forensic-evidence.

3. According to The Centers for Disease Control and Prevention, women aged 20-24 years old experience the highest rates of intimate partner violence[5].

If you are being physically attacked, it is important to take immediate action to protect yourself. Here are some steps to follow:

1. Get away from the attacker: If possible, run away from the attacker to a place where there are other people and call for help.

2. Use your voice: Yell, scream, and make as much noise as possible to attract attention and deter the attacker.

3. Use self-defense techniques: If you have undergone self-defense training, use the techniques you have learned to defend yourself. Aim for vulnerable areas such as the eyes, nose, and throat.

4. Call 911: Dial emergency services as soon as possible. Provide them with your location and describe the attacker.

5. Stay safe: Once you have escaped the attacker, find a safe place and do not return to the scene of the attack until law enforcement has arrived.

Verbal Harassment:

1. A 2019 survey by Stop Street Harassment found that 81% of women in the US have experienced some form of street harassment[6].

5. National Center for Injury Prevention and Control (NCIPC), Centers for Disease Control and Prevention (CDC). (2011). National Intimate Partner and Sexual Violence Survey. Retrieved from https://www.cdc.gov/violenceprevention/pdf/nisvs _report2010-a.pdf.

6. Stop Street Harassment. (n.d.). National Studies. Retrieved from https://stopstre etharassment.org/our-work/nationalstudy/.

2. A 2015 study by the American Association of University Women found that 66% of 7th-12th grade students in the US reported experiencing gender-based harassment[7].

3. A 2019 report by the National Women's Law Center found that nearly 2 in 3 women of color in the US reported experiencing harassment in the workplace[8].

Verbal harassment can be a traumatic and stressful experience. Here are tips that can help you deal with it:

1. Remove yourself from the situation: If possible, leave the area where the harassment is taking place.

2. Speak up: If you feel it is safe to do so, confidently assert yourself and say that the behavior is not okay.

3. Seek support: Talk to someone you trust about the experience, like a friend, family member, or a support group.

4. Document the incidents: Keep a record of the incidents, including what was said and who was present.

5. Report the harassment: If the harassment continues, consider reporting it to the appropriate authorities, such as the police or your employer.

It's important to remember that you're not alone and that help is available. Don't be afraid to reach out for support.

---

7. American Association of University Women (AAUW). (n.d.). Research. Retrieved from https://www.aauw.org/research/.

8. National Women's Law Center (NWLC). (n.d.). Workplace harassment. Retrieved from https://nwlc.org/issue/sexual-harassment-in-the-workplace/.

Stalking:

1. According to the National Center for Victims of Crime, nearly 1 in 6 women in the US will be stalked in their lifetime[9].

2. The National Intimate Partner and Sexual Violence Survey 2016/2017 reported that 43.4% of stalking victims reported being stalked by a current or former intimate partner[10].

3. A 2020 study by the National Institute of Justice found that stalking victims were 3 times more likely to experience violence from their stalkers compared to those not being stalked[11].

To prevent and deal with stalking, it's important to trust your instincts and take any threats seriously. Here are some tips for staying safe:

1. Keep records: Keep a record of all incidents, including dates, times, and any evidence such as emails, messages, or pictures.

2. Take legal action: Get a restraining order if necessary.

3. Use technology: Technology such as call-blocking or GPS-enabled devices can help you protect yourself.

4. Reach out for help: Tell friends, family, and co-workers about the situation and seek their support.

5. Call the authorities: Inform law enforcement and seek their assistance.

9. National Center for Victims of Crime. (n.d.). Stalking Resource Center. Retrieved from https://victimsofcrime.org/stalking-resource-center/.

10. , Centers of Disease Control and Prevention. (April 2022). 2016/2017 Report on Stalking. https://www.cdc.gov/violenceprevention/pdf/nisvs/ nisvsStalkingReport.pdf.

11. National Institute of Justice (NIJ). (October 24, 2007). Overview of Stalking.

In case of an active stalking situation, it's crucial to:

1. Get to safety: Stay in a public place or with someone you trust.

2. Trust your instincts: Listen to your gut and take immediate action if you feel threatened.

3. Call the authorities: Call 911 or local emergency services.

4. Keep your phone with you: Make sure your phone is always charged and easily accessible.

The National Institute of Justice (NIJ) states that in the US, 1 in 6 women and 1 in 19 men have been stalked at some point in their lives. It's important to take stalking seriously and take steps to protect yourself.

Domestic Violence:

1. The National Domestic Violence Hotline reported that in 2020, they received an average of 1.07 calls per minute or 636,968 calls, chats, and texts, seeking help for domestic violence[12].

2. The National Coalition Against Domestic Violence found that, on average, 20 people per minute are physically abused by an intimate partner in the US[13].

Domestic violence is a serious issue that affects many women in the US. To stay safe, it's important to understand the warning signs of abuse and have a plan in place for getting help. Here are some tips to keep in mind:

1. Know the warning signs of abuse: Physical violence, threats of violence, control-

---

12. National Domestic Violence Hotline. (n.d.). 2020 A Year of Impact. https://www.thehotline.org/wp-content/uploads/media/2021/06/ Hotline-EOY-Impact-Report-2020.pdf.

13. National Coalition Against Domestic Violence (NCADV). (n.d.). Statistics. Retrieved from https://ncadv.org/statistics.

ling behavior, and intimidation are all signs of domestic abuse.

2. Have a safety plan in place: This could include having a trusted friend or family member to call in case of an emergency, keeping important documents and money with you, and knowing the location of the nearest domestic violence shelter.

3. Reach out for help: There are many resources available to help victims of domestic violence, including hotlines, support groups, and counseling services.

4. Document the abuse: Keeping a record of incidents can help you build a case if you decide to pursue legal action.

5. Trust your instincts: If you feel that you're in danger, it's important to take action to protect yourself.

6. Don't stay silent: Talking about the abuse with trusted friends and family can help you get the support you need to escape a dangerous situation.

If you are a victim of domestic violence, it is important to seek help as soon as possible. You can reach out to the National Domestic Violence Hotline (1-800-799-7233) or a local domestic violence organization for support and resources. You can also contact law enforcement for immediate assistance. It is important to have a safety plan in place, such as having a place to go if you need to leave your home, keeping important documents and belongings in a safe location, and saving contact information for trusted friends and family members. Remember, domestic violence is never your fault, and help is available.

Carjacking:

1. The FBI reported that in 2019, there were nearly 5,000 carjackings in the US[14].

---

14. Federal Bureau of Investigation (FBI). (n.d.). Crime in the U.S. 2019. Retrieved from .

2. A 2022 study by the National Crime Victimization Survey found that the majority of carjacking involved someone with a weapon (59%[15].

Carjackings happen when someone takes a car from its owner by force, usually through violence or the threat of violence.

To reduce the risk of carjacking:

1. Be aware: Keep an eye on your surroundings and stay alert while driving or approaching your car.

2. Lock up: Keep doors locked and windows closed while driving.

3. Park in bright areas: Avoid parking in isolated or poorly lit areas.

4. Keep valuables hidden: Avoid displaying valuable items in the car.

5. Stay alert: Be cautious of anyone following you or approaching your car.

6. Trust your instincts: Pay attention if you feel unsafe and take action if you feel threatened.

In case of a carjacking:

1. Keep calm: Do not resist if a carjacker threatens violence.

2. Document the incident: Try to remember details about the attacker and the vehicle for later identification.

3. Call the authorities: Call the police as soon as it's safe to do so and provide them with all the information you have.

4. Get to safety: If you are able to escape, do so immediately and seek help from a trusted friend, family member or law enforcement.

---

15. U.S. Department of Justice, Bureau of Justice Statistics (BJS). (October 2022). Just the Stats, Carjacking Victimization, 1995-2021. Retrieved from https://bjs.ojp.go v/carjacking-victimization-1995-2021.

5. Don't make a pursuit: Do not attempt to follow the attacker or retrieve your vehicle. Your safety is more important than your car.

Note: The best way to reduce the risk of carjacking is to take preventative measures and be aware of your surroundings at all times.

Mugging:

1. A 2020 study by the National Crime Victimization Survey found that mugging victims were more likely to be younger adults, particularly males between the ages of 18-34[16].

2. The FBI reported that in 2019, there were over 260,000 robberies in the US[17].

To stay safe and prevent or escape a mugging:

1. Stay alert: Be aware of your surroundings and trust your instincts. If a situation feels dangerous, it probably is.

2. Walk in brightly lit areas: Avoid walking or standing in isolated or dark areas, especially at night.

3. Protect your valuables: Keep your valuables and cash out of sight and carry only what you need.

4. Don't be flashy: Avoid wearing expensive jewelry or carrying large amounts of cash.

5. Trust your instincts: If you feel like you're being followed, change direction or cross the street.

6.

---

16. U.S. Department of Justice, Bureau of Justice Statistics (BJS). (October 2021). Criminal Victimization, 2020. Retrieved from .

17. Federal Bureau of Investigation (FBI). (n.d.). Robbery. Retrieved from https://uc r.fbi.gov/crime-in-the-u.s/2019/crime-in-the-u.s.-2019/topic-pages/robbery.

Don't resist: If someone demands your valuables, hand them over without resistance. Your safety is more important than your possessions.

7. Use self-defense: If you are physically attacked, try to defend yourself using pepper spray or a personal alarm.

8. Report the incident: Report the mugging to the police as soon as possible. Try to remember as many details about the attacker as possible, such as clothing, height, and any unique features.

According to the FBI's Uniform Crime Reporting (UCR) Program, there were approximately 267,988 mugging offenses reported in the United States in 2019[18]. This is a decrease from previous years, but it's still important to stay aware and take precautions to prevent becoming a victim.

Sexual Assault:

1. The RAINN (Rape, Abuse & Incest National Network) reported that every 68 seconds, an American is sexually assaulted[19].

2. A 2017 study by the National Intimate Partner and Sexual Violence Survey found that nearly 2 in 5 women in the US have experienced sexual violence in their lifetime[20].

18. Federal Bureau of Investigation (FBI). (n.d.). Robbery. Retrieved from https://ucr.fbi.gov/crime-in-the-u.s/2019/crime-in-the-u.s.-2019/topic-pages/robbery.

19. Rape, Abuse & Incest National Network (RAINN). (n.d.). Statistics. Retrieved from https://www.rainn.org/statistics.

20. The National Intimate Partner and Sexual Violence Survey (NISVS), Centers of Disease Control and Prevention. (October 2022). 2016/2017 Report on Intimate Partner Violence. Retrieved from https://www.cdc.gov/violenceprevention/pdf/nisvs/nisvsreportonipv_2022.pdf.

Sexual assault is a serious crime and can have long-lasting effects on a person's physical and emotional well-being. Here are some tips for staying safe and what to do if you become a victim:

1. Trust your instincts: If a situation feels uncomfortable, remove yourself as quickly and safely as possible.

2. Be aware of your surroundings: Pay attention to who is around you and what is going on. Avoid walking or jogging alone in isolated areas, especially at night.

3. Avoid alcohol and drugs: Substance abuse can impair your judgment and increase your risk of becoming a victim.

4. Know self-defense techniques: Consider taking a self-defense class to learn techniques to protect yourself in an emergency situation.

5. Report the assault: If you are a victim of sexual assault, it is important to report it to the police as soon as possible. This will increase the chances of the perpetrator being caught and can help provide evidence for a criminal case.

6. Seek medical attention: Get a medical examination as soon as possible after the assault, even if you do not have any visible injuries. A doctor can test for sexually transmitted infections, provide emergency contraception, and offer other medical services.

7. Get support: Consider reaching out to a rape crisis center or a trusted friend or family member for emotional support. Talking to someone about what happened can help you process your feelings and cope with trauma.

According to the National Sexual Violence Resource Center, 1 in 5 women in the US will be sexually assaulted in their lifetime[21]. It is estimated that only 310 out of every 1,000 sexual assaults are reported to the police[22].

• • • ● • ● • • • •

Be Prepared for Anything (Including a Zombie Apocalypse)

 Having a first aid kit at home or in your car can be of essential help in emergency situations. A well-stocked first aid kit should include the following items:

1. Adhesive bandages of various sizes

2. Antiseptic wipes or solution

3. Sterile gauze pads and adhesive tape

4. Tweezers

5. Scissors

6. Pain relievers (e.g., acetaminophen, ibuprofen)

7. Instant cold pack

8. CPR breathing barrier (such as a face shield)

9. Gloves

---

21. National Sexual Violence Resource Center (NSVRC). (n.d.). Sexual Assault Statistics. Retrieved from https://www.nsvrc.org/statistics.

22. Rape, Abuse & Incest National Network (RAINN). (n.d.). The Criminal Justice System: Statistics. Retrieved from https://www.rainn.org/statistics/criminal-justice-system.

10. First aid manual

In addition to these basic items, consider including other items specific to your needs, such as medication, an epinephrine auto-injector (for severe allergies), and any special equipment for specific medical conditions.

Having a first aid kit on hand can help you treat minor injuries quickly and properly. It is also a good idea to periodically check the contents of the kit and replace any expired or used items.

What to Do In Case Of...

- **Burns:**

1. Assess the severity of the burn: Determine the degree of the burn based on skin color, pain, and size. First-degree burns are mild and cause redness, second-degree burns cause blistering and swelling, and third-degree burns are severe and result in white or charred skin.

2. Cool the burn: If the burn is less than three inches in diameter, immerse it in cool water for 10 to 15 minutes. This will help reduce pain and prevent further tissue damage.

3. Remove any clothing or jewelry near the burn: Clothing and jewelry can trap heat and make the burn worse, so it's important to remove them if possible.

4. Clean the burn: Gently wash the burn with soap and water to remove dirt and debris. Do not use hydrogen peroxide or alcohol, as these can damage the skin.

5. Apply a sterile bandage: Cover the burn with a sterile gauze bandage or wrap it in a clean cloth to prevent infection. Do not use adhesive bandages or ointments, as these can trap heat and make the burn worse.

6. Take pain relievers: Over-the-counter pain relievers such as ibuprofen or acetaminophen can reduce pain and swelling.

7. Seek medical attention: If the burn is larger than three inches in diameter; if it's

a second or third-degree burn; or if it's on the face, hands, feet, or a major joint; seek medical attention. A doctor may prescribe antibiotics or other treatments to prevent infection and promote healing.

- **Cuts:**

Cuts are common injuries that can happen at home, at work, or outdoors. To treat a cut:

1. Clean the affected area: Rinse the cut under running water to remove any dirt or debris.

2. Stop the bleeding: Apply gentle pressure to the cut with a clean cloth or bandage until the bleeding stops.

3. Apply antiseptic: Use an antiseptic solution or ointment to prevent infection.

4. Cover the cut: Cover the cut with a sterile adhesive bandage or wrap it with sterile gauze.

5. Monitor for signs of infection: Watch for signs of infection such as redness, swelling, or increased pain. If the cut becomes infected, seek medical attention.

Note: If the cut is deep, the edges are jagged, or the bleeding won't stop, seek immediate medical attention.

- **Broken Bones:**

To deal with a broken bone, follow these steps:

1. Call for emergency medical assistance: Dial 911 or the local emergency number.

2. Protect the injured limb or joint: Avoid moving the bone if possible, as this can cause additional damage.

3. Stabilize the bone: Apply a splint or improvised support, such as a rolled-up magazine or cardboard.

4. Apply ice: Apply ice to the injured area to reduce swelling and pain.

5. Stay calm: Keep the injured person still and comfortable until medical help arrives.

It is important to seek medical attention for a broken bone as soon as possible, as some bones may need to be realigned through manipulation or surgery. If broken bones aren't taken care of properly, they can cause long-term problems like reduced mobility or chronic pain.

- **Fainting:**

If you or someone else faints:

1. Call for emergency help: Call for emergency medical services if necessary.

2. Lie down: Lay the person down on their back, elevate their legs higher than their heart, and loosen any tight clothing

3. Check breathing: Check the person's airway, breathing, and pulse to make sure that they are still conscious and breathing.

4. Stay still: If the person is unconscious or having a seizure, do not move them unless it is necessary to keep them safe.

5. Keep cool: Help the person stay cool with a fan or a damp cloth and offer water if they are conscious and able to drink.

6. Stay in place: Wait for emergency medical services to arrive and follow their instructions.

- **Choking:**

To help someone who is choking, perform the Heimlich Maneuver:

1. Stand behind the person and slightly to one side.

2. Wrap your arms around their waist and make a fist with one hand.

3. Locate the person's navel with the thumb of your other hand.

4. Quickly thrust inward and upward into the person's abdomen.

5. Repeat the thrusts until the object is dislodged.

6. If the person becomes unconscious, call emergency services and start CPR.

Note: Do not attempt these steps if the person is still able to cough, speak, or breathe. It is recommended to take a CPR course to learn the proper technique.

- **Drowning:**

Drowning is a serious and life-threatening emergency that requires immediate attention. If you witness someone drowning or you yourself are struggling in water, follow these steps:

1. Call for help: If you have access to a phone, dial 911 immediately and explain the situation to the operator. If you are unable to call for help, try to signal someone nearby to come to your aid.

2. Reach or throw: If you are near a person who is drowning, reach out to them with a long object like a stick or rope to try and pull them to safety. If you are unable to reach them, try throwing them something buoyant like a life jacket or pool noodle.

3. Go for the person: If you are a strong swimmer and able to do so safely, go to the person and attempt to bring them to safety. Make sure to keep yourself safe while doing this.

4. Perform CPR: If the person is unconscious and not breathing, perform CPR immediately.

- **Zombie Apocalypse:**

Dealing with a zombie apocalypse requires a combination of preparedness and quick thinking. Here are some tips to help you survive:

1.

Stock up on essential supplies: Make sure you have plenty of food, water, medicine, and other essentials. You may also want to consider purchasing weapons, ammunition, and other defense tools.

2. Find a safe place: Look for a secure location that is easy to defend, has plenty of resources, and is relatively free from zombies. This could be a house, apartment building, or even a large vehicle.

3. Form a group: Joining forces with other survivors is a great way to increase your chances of survival. Make sure you choose people you can trust who have similar goals complement each other's skills.

4. Stay informed: Keep track of the latest news and information about the zombie outbreak. This will help you make informed decisions and respond to new threats.

5. Protect yourself: Wear protective clothing, such as gloves and a mask, to reduce your exposure to zombies. Be prepared to defend yourself using weapons and other tools.

6. Stay alert: Always be aware of your surroundings and be ready to react quickly if a zombie appears. Keep your wits about you and don't let your guard down.

7. Have a plan: Make sure you have a clear plan for how you will respond in different scenarios. This will help you stay organized and focused even when things get chaotic.

Well, we've covered some heavy stuff! From personal safety to first aid to natural disasters. But let's be real, all that information can be overwhelming. That's why I want to move on to a lighter note and talk about happiness and mental health. Day-to-day adulting and mental well-being may seem like unrelated topics, but when you think about it, feeling secure and having the tools to help yourself and others go hand-in-hand with feeling happy and fulfilled. So let's take a step back, take a deep breath, and jump into the next chapter with a positive outlook.

Chapter Seven

Stay Happy and Alive

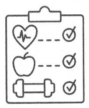

M ENTAL HEALTH IS JUST as important as physical health, and it's something that we often neglect in the hustle and bustle of daily life, especially when adulting on our own for the first time.

The National Institute of Mental Health (NIMH) says that women are more likely than men to have depression[1], and about 1 in 8 women will have depression at some point in their lives[2]. A paper in the journal Brain and Behavior showed that women are twice as likely as men to experience anxiety[3].

1. National Institute of Mental Health (NIMH). (May 2021). Women and Mental Health. Retrieved from https://www.nimh.nih.gov/health/topics/women-and-mental-health.

These figures show how important it is for people, especially women, to pay attention to their mental health and get help when they need it.

That's why it's crucial to make self-care a priority and pay attention to your mental well-being. This can include doing things that make you happy and help you relax, living a healthy lifestyle, and getting help when you need it from friends, family, or mental health professionals.

So, let's not forget that taking care of our mental health is an essential part of adulting, and it's never too late to start prioritizing it!

Here are a few habits to help you be at your best, both mentally and physically:

Get good sleep:

Getting enough good-quality sleep is important for physical and mental well-being.

- **Go outside:**
  Spending time in nature has been shown to improve mood and reduce stress.

- **Practice safe sex:**
  Protect yourself against sexually transmitted infections (STIs) and unwanted pregnancy.

- **Wear sunscreen:**
  Protecting skin from harmful UV rays helps prevent skin cancer and other skin damage.

- **Don't smoke:**
  Smoking is the leading risk factor for many types of cancer and heart disease.

- **Cook more and eat out less:**
  Cooking at home allows you to control what ingredients are used and can lead to healthier eating habits.

- **Eat fruits and vegetables of many different colors:**
  A diet full of varied fruits and vegetables gives your body the nutrients it needs

to stay healthy.

- **Quit drinking soda:**
  Drinking soda can cause you to eat more calories, gain weight, and have a higher chance of getting sick.

- **Drink more water:**
  Staying hydrated is important for your overall health and can also help with weight management.

- **Keep moving and sit less:**
  Regular physical activity is important for maintaining physical and mental health.

- **Be grateful:**
  Practicing gratitude can improve your mood and increase feelings of well-being.

- **Be mindful:**
  Mindfulness practices, such as meditation, can help reduce stress and improve mental well-being.

- **Stay away from toxic people:**
  Surrounding oneself with positive, supportive people can have a significant impact on mental health.

- **Limit alcohol consumption:**
  Excessive alcohol consumption can lead to health problems and negative impacts on mental well-being.

- **Practice stress-management techniques:**
  Managing stress through activities such as meditation or yoga can improve mental health.

- **Stay connected with friends and family:**
  Social support is important for mental well-being.

- **Volunteer or give back to the community:**

Helping others can increase feelings of purpose and satisfaction.

- **Find a creative outlet:**
  Engaging in creative activities can reduce stress and improve mental well-being.

- **Get regular check-ups with a doctor and dentist:**
  Regular check-ups can help prevent, detect, and treat health problems early on.

- **Take breaks throughout the day to stretch and move:**
  Taking breaks from sitting can improve physical and mental health.

Big Emotions

"Big emotions" refers to intense feelings, such as anger, sadness, fear, or joy, that can have a significant impact on our well-being. These emotions can be triggered by events in our lives, such as the loss of a loved one, a job change, or a relationship challenge.

Handling big feelings is an important skill, and it's important to learn how to recognize and manage symptoms of mental health challenges. For example, persistent feelings of sadness and hopelessness may be a sign of depression. Intense feelings of worry or fear may be a sign of an anxiety disorder. Chronic stress can lead to physical health problems, such as heart disease or digestive issues.

It's important to recognize and address big emotions, as ignoring them can make them worse over time. It's also helpful to learn healthy ways to cope with big feelings in healthy and effective ways, like talking to a trusted friend, getting some exercise, or getting help from a professional.

• • • ● • ● • ● • •

The Wheel of Feelings

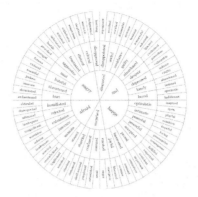

The "Wheel of Feelings" is a visual tool that can help people figure out what they are feeling and why. Usually, the wheel is a circle with different sections that each represent a different emotion. You can find tons of examples and images of the wheel on Google.

The idea behind the Wheel of Feelings is that emotions are often interconnected and complex. For example, while feeling sad, we may also feel lonely or frustrated. The Wheel of Feelings can help people learn more about their feelings and understand them better by helping them visualize the different emotions that they are feeling in a given situation.

In order to use the Wheel of Feelings effectively, it's important to define the different emotions correctly. For example, anger is different from frustration, and joy is different from excitement. Understanding the differences between these feelings can help people come up with better ways to deal with them and talk about how they feel.

Here's a story to illustrate the usefulness of the Wheel of Feelings:

A woman named Sarah was feeling overwhelmed and didn't know why. She went to see a therapist, who suggested she use the Wheel of Feelings to identify what she was feeling. Sarah was surprised to realize that she was feeling not just overwhelmed, but also sad, frustrated, and scared. With this new information, Sarah and her therapist were able to come up with good ways for her to deal with her feelings and move forward in a healthy way.

In short, the Wheel of Feelings is a helpful tool for people who want to learn more about their emotions. By classifying and defining emotions, individuals can make better decisions, communicate more effectively, and develop healthier coping strategies.

• • • ● • ● • • • •

Cognitive Behavioral Therapy (CBT)

Cognitive Behavioral Therapy (CBT) is a type of psychotherapy that helps people recognize and change negative patterns of thinking and acting. CBT is based on the idea that our thoughts, emotions, and behaviors are interconnected and that by changing the way we think, we can change the way we feel and behave.

CBT can help people deal with hard feelings because it helps them figure out and change negative thought patterns that might be making them feel bad. People can learn new ways to deal with problems and develop healthier ways of thinking and acting by using CBT.

In CBT, limiting beliefs are defined as negative, fixed thoughts that make it hard for a person to live a full, happy life. Some common types of limiting beliefs that CBT addresses include:

1. **All-or-nothing thinking:**
   Believing that everything is either black or white with no grey area in between. *"If I don't get an A on this exam, I'm a complete failure."* Using CBT, you might learn to challenge this thought by looking for evidence that supports a more balanced view. For example, you could consider past successes, positive qualities you possess, or your efforts to prepare for the exam.

2. **Overgeneralization:**
   Drawing broad conclusions from a single negative experience. *"I've been rejected by one person, so no one will ever like me."* CBT can help you challenge this thought by having you look for evidence that refutes it. For example, you might consider past experiences where you have been liked or accepted or think about people in your life who do like you.

3. Mental filtering:

Focusing on the negative aspects of a situation and disregarding the positives. *"Everything about this situation is terrible. There is no silver lining."* You can challenge this thought with CBT by deliberately looking for and focusing on positive experiences, no matter how small. For example, you might make a gratitude journal or practice mindfulness meditation to bring awareness to the present moment.

4. Disqualifying the positive:

Dismissing positive experiences or accomplishments as insignificant or mean-ingless. *"That's not a real accomplishment, anyone could have done it."* CBT can help you fight this thought by having you point out the good things in your life, no matter how small. For example, you might make a list of your achievements or ask a trusted friend or family member for their perspective.

5. Mind reading:

Assuming you know what others are thinking or feeling without any concrete evidence. *"They're angry with me because I said that."* CBT can help you challenge this thought by having you look for evidence that supports or refutes it. For example, you might ask the person directly if they're upset or consider other possible explanations for their behavior.

6. Fortune-telling:

Predicting the future in a negative way without any evidence. *"I just know that this is going to turn out badly."* You can challenge this thought with CBT by focusing on what is happening in the present moment, rather than trying to predict the future. For example, you might engage in positive self-talk or focus on your coping skills and resources that have helped in the past.

7. Emotional reasoning:

Believing that your feelings accurately reflect reality. *"I feel it, so it must be true."* CBT can help you challenge this thought by having you separate emotions from facts. For example, you might make a list of pros and cons, or you might ask yourself, "What would I tell a friend in this situation?"

8.

"Should" statements:

Believing that there is a strict set of rules that dictate how you or others should behave. *"I should be able to handle this."* You can challenge this thought with CBT by recognizing that perfectionism is unrealistic and unhelpful. For example, you might try to reframe "should" statements as preferences or desires, or you can practice self-compassion by acknowledging your efforts and growth.

9. **Control fallacies:**

Believing that you can control everything in and around you. *"I should be able to control my own emotions."* CBT can help you challenge this thought by teaching you to recognize that emotions are a natural and normal part of being human and that it's okay to not always be in control. For example, you might engage in self-compassion practices like self-talk, journaling, or visualization.

10. **Fairness fallacies:**

Believing that things should happen based on perceived fairness. *"It's not fair that they have it better than I do."* CBT can help you challenge this thought by having you look for evidence that supports a more balanced perspective. For example, you might consider the advantages and disadvantages of both situations or focus on your own strengths and abilities.

11. **Blame:**

Assigning blame to others for things that happen. *"It's all their fault that I'm feeling this way."* You can use CBT to challenge this thought by recognizing your own role in creating your emotions and experiences. For example, you might consider your thoughts, behaviors, and reactions and use this knowledge to take responsibility for your own happiness and well-being.

12. **Personalization:**

Assigning blame to yourself for things you can't control. *"It's my fault that my friend is upset."* CBT can help you challenge this thought by teaching you to look for external factors that might have contributed to the situation. For example, you might consider your friend's mood, external stressors, or other variables that could have played a role in your friend's upset.

In CBT, you can learn to recognize and question false beliefs, then replace them with more realistic and healthy ones. This can help you feel more empowered and in control of your emotions, leading to improved well-being.

I have included a very useful "Thought Record" in the free Adulting Hard Workbook. This will help you record and process any big emotions that come up and sabotage you. Just visit https://adultinghardbooks.com to download it.

• • • ● ●• ● ● • • ·

Now... Breathe

Mindful breathing is a simple yet powerful tool for improving mental health. When practiced regularly, it can help reduce stress, anxiety, and depression while promoting a sense of calm and relaxation.

Some benefits of mindful breathing include:

1. **Reduces stress and anxiety:**
   By focusing on the present moment and breathing deeply, mindful breathing can help to release tension and reduce feelings of stress and anxiety.

2. **Improves mood:**
   Mindful breathing has been shown to activate the parasympathetic nervous system, which promotes feelings of calm and relaxation.

3. **Increases self-awareness:**
   Mindful breathing can help you become more aware of your thoughts, feelings, and bodily sensations, allowing you to gain a better understanding of yourself and your emotional state.

4. **Boosts cognitive function:**
   By reducing stress and promoting relaxation, mindful breathing can improve cognitive function, including memory, focus, and creativity.

5. **Enhances physical health:**
   Practicing mindful breathing regularly has been linked to a number of physical health benefits, including lower blood pressure, improved sleep quality, and enhanced immune function.

Mindful breathing is a great way to improve your mental health, help you relax, and improve your overall well-being.

Here are some of the most popular mindful breathing techniques to promote relaxation and reduce stress and anxiety:

- **4-7-8 Breathing:**
  Inhale for 4 counts, hold your breath for 7 counts, then exhale for 8 counts.

- **Box Breathing:**
  Breathe in for 4 counts, hold your breath for 4 counts, exhale for 4 counts, then hold your breath again for 4 counts. This technique helps to calm the mind and body.

- **Progressive Muscle Relaxation:**
  Begin by tensing a specific muscle group, such as your feet, for 5-10 seconds, then relax and focus on the sensation of relaxation for 10-20 seconds. Repeat this process for each muscle group.

- **Alternate Nostril Breathing:**
  Close one nostril and inhale deeply through the other nostril, then switch which nostril you are holding and exhale through the other nostril. This technique can help balance the body.

- **Belly Breathing:**
  Place one hand on your stomach and one hand on your chest, then breathe deeply into your diaphragm, allowing your stomach to rise and fall.

It's important to remember that when practicing breathing techniques, it's helpful to find a quiet and relaxed environment and to focus solely on your breathing. Focusing on your breath for a few minutes can help you feel less stressed and more relaxed, which is good for your mental health.

Ommmm

The power of meditation lies in its ability to quiet the mind, reduce stress and anxiety, and promote a sense of inner peace and calm. It has been shown to be good for both your physical and mental health in many ways, such as reducing inflammation, improving sleep quality, and easing depression and anxiety.

Some common misconceptions surrounding meditation include the belief that it is difficult or that one must be spiritual to practice it. However, meditation can be as simple as taking a few minutes each day to focus on your breathing and bring awareness to the present moment. Meditation can be practiced by anyone, regardless of spiritual beliefs or religion.

Here are some of the most popular meditation techniques:

- **Body Scan Meditation:**
  This technique involves lying down or sitting comfortably and focusing on each part of your body, from your toes to the crown of your head, taking care to notice all sensations and release tension from your body.

- **Mindfulness Meditation:**
  This technique involves bringing your awareness to the present moment, focusing on your breath, and observing your thoughts and emotions without judgment.

- **Loving-Kindness Meditation:**
  This technique involves sending positive thoughts and well wishes to yourself, your loved ones, and eventually to all beings.

- **Mantra Meditation**:

  This technique involves repeating a word or phrase, such as "peace" or "calm", to quiet your mind and bring focus to the present moment.

- **Guided Meditation:**

  This technique involves listening to a recorded meditation led by a guide to bring focus and relaxation to your mind and body.

It's important to find a quiet, relaxed environment and to set aside a few minutes each day for meditation. By making meditation a part of your daily life, you can enjoy its many benefits for your physical and mental health.

I have included a "Daily Wellness Log" in the free Adulting Hard Workbook to help you track your affirmations, thoughts, and reflections throughout the day. Just visit https://adultinghardbooks.com to download it.

• • • ● • ● • • •

The Wild World of Health Insurance

Hold onto your wallet! Welcome to the wild, wild world of American healthcare, where the bills are high and the options are low... Well, actually, the options are plentiful, but they're all so confusing that they might as well be low.

But fear not because, as the great philosopher Ferris Bueller once said, "Life moves pretty fast. If you don't stop and look around once in a while, you could miss it." And we don't want you to miss out on the best health insurance options, so let's dive in!

Let's say you're a single woman in the prime of your life, looking to secure your healthcare for the future. You've got a few options to choose from: employer-sponsored insurance, individual plans purchased through the marketplace, Medicaid, and Medicare. You might also continue to stay on your parents' policy until you turn 26.

Each option has its pros and cons, and choosing the right one for you will depend on factors such as your income, age, and health status. It's like dating; you want to find the one that's going to make you feel secure, won't break the bank, and has all the right benefits (pun intended).

Health insurance can seem like a foreign language, but don't worry, I'm here to help you understand it!

Here are the definitions of some common terms you're likely to run into:

Premium: A premium is like a monthly membership fee you pay to have health insurance coverage.

Deductible: A deductible is what you pay for your health expenses before your insurance starts covering your costs. Once it's met, your insurance will start chipping in.

Copay: A copay is a small fee you pay each time you visit the doctor, like a cover charge at a club.

Out-of-pocket Maximum: The out-of-pocket maximum is like a spending limit for your healthcare expenses in a year. Once you reach that amount, your insurance will cover the rest.

Network: A network is a group of healthcare providers that your insurance has agreed to cover. It's like having a VIP pass to specific hospitals and doctors.

When it comes to health insurance, there are three main types of plans: PPO, HMO, and HSA. Let's break down what each of these acronyms means:

PPO, or Preferred Provider Organization:
A PPO allows you to see any doctor or specialist within their network without a referral, but you'll likely pay more out-of-pocket if you see a doctor outside the network. Think of a PPO like a big all-you-can-eat buffet: you have a lot of options to choose from, but they might cost a bit more.

HMO, or Health Maintenance Organization:
An HMO typically requires you to choose a primary care physician who acts as a gate-

keeper to any specialists you might need to see. You'll pay less out-of-pocket if you stay within the HMO network, but you'll likely need a referral to see a specialist. Think of an HMO like a pre-set menu at a restaurant: you have limited options, but everything is included in the price.

HSA, or Health Savings Account:
An HSA is a type of savings account that you can use to pay for qualified medical expenses. You can only enroll in an HSA if you have a high-deductible health plan. Think of an HSA as a piggy bank specifically for your health expenses: you put money in it, and you can use that money to pay for healthcare costs.

Medicaid:
Medicaid is a federally and state-funded health insurance program that provides coverage to low-income individuals. Medicaid can be a good option if you don't have health insurance through your employer, but you'll have to check whether you are eligible in your state.

Medicare:
Medicare is a federal health insurance program for those who are 65 or older, although younger individuals receiving disability benefits for chronic conditions may qualify as well. Although you might not need Medicare just yet, it can't hurt to know what it's all about!

Each of these options has pros and cons, so it's important to carefully consider which one is right for you based on your individual needs and budget.

See, that wasn't so bad, was it? You're now a pro at decoding the language of health insurance!

There are a few things to consider before you make your decision on which health insurance option is right for you.

If you're a young, healthy individual with low healthcare needs, a plan with a high deductible and low premium might be the way to go. This means you'll pay less each month but more out-of-pocket if you do need to see a doctor.

If you have a pre-existing condition or expect to need frequent medical care, a plan with a lower deductible and higher premium might be a better fit. This means you'll pay more each month but spend less out-of-pocket when you see a doctor.

If you're on a tight budget, Medicaid or a marketplace plan with subsidies based on your income might be the way to go.

If you're over 65, you'll want to look into Medicare options, and you probably shouldn't be reading this book... Haha!

And lastly, don't forget to consider your personal preferences. Do you want a plan with a wider network of providers, or are you okay with seeing a limited selection of doctors? Do you want a plan that covers certain procedures, like acupuncture or mental health services, or are you looking for just the basics?

The most important thing is to find a plan that fits your individual needs and budget. It's like finding the perfect pair of shoes—it might take a little time, but when you find the right one, it's worth it.

CHAPTER EIGHT

THE MOST INTERESTING WOMAN IN THE WORLD

S O, YOU WANT TO be the most interesting woman in the world, huh? Or, at the very least, in the room. Well, buckle up because we're about to embark on an epic journey to become a Renaissance woman!

Before we dive in, let's get one thing straight: being interesting doesn't mean being a know-it-all or a walking encyclopedia. It's about having a wide range of interests, skills, and hobbies and being able to share those passions with others in an engaging and relatable way.

Think of it like this: have you ever been at a party and ended up talking to that one person who acted like they just knew everything about everything? Before you knew it, you were checking your watch, hoping that the conversation would end soon. Yeah, we don't want that to be you. Instead, we want you to be the person that everyone seeks out, eager to chat and learn more about your unique interests and experiences.

So let's get to it! And remember, the key to being the most interesting woman in the room is to have fun and be yourself.

• • • ● • ● • • •

Journal Your Life

I remember this night like it was yesterday. I was in my late twenties, and I had just met a fascinating woman at a cocktail party. We chatted for hours about our travels, favorite books, and the most memorable moments of our lives. As she walked away, I thought to myself, "Wow, I want to be like her." She was confident, well-spoken, and had an endless supply of interesting stories to tell.

That's when I realized that I needed a way to keep track of my own experiences and the amazing people I met along the way. And so, I started a list called **"Cool Things I've Done and People I've Met."** It was just a simple Word document, but it quickly became my go-to whenever I wanted to recall a memory or share a story.

As the years went by, I added to the list, jotting down the highlights of my life: the skydiving trip I took in my thirties, the time I flew in a fighter jet, and the concert I attended that left me in awe. And when I was at a party or meeting someone new, I would often pull out the list and flip through the pages, reliving those moments and reigniting my enthusiasm for life.

And that's what journaling can do for you, too. By taking the time to reflect on your experiences and document the things that excite you, you'll have a rich tapestry of stories to share with others, and you'll never be at a loss for words. So go ahead, grab a notebook, and start writing down your own "Cool Things I've Done and People I've Met" list. You'll be able to look back at that list and forever be amazed by the memories you've created and the connections you've made.

• • • ● • ● • • •

Go Places!

Travel is one of the greatest gifts you can give yourself. It broadens your horizons, exposes you to new cultures and ways of life, and helps you grow as a person. And, don't forget, it's also a lot of fun!

With that in mind, I've put together a list of the Top 10 Places Every Woman Should Visit. These destinations will challenge you, inspire you, and leave you with memories that will last a lifetime.

1. **Tokyo, Japan** - With its cutting-edge technology, delicious cuisine, and vibrant culture, Tokyo is a must-visit destination for anyone looking to experience the future and immerse themselves in a new way of life. Must-sees include the breathtaking Tokyo Skytree, the bustling Shibuya Crossing, and the peaceful temples of Asakusa.

2. **Paris, France** - The city of love and lights is a haven for those who appreciate art, fashion, and history. Stroll along the Champs-Élysées, admire the stunning architecture of the Louvre Museum and indulge in the city's renowned patisseries and boulangeries.

3. **Marrakech, Morocco** - This vibrant city will transport you to another world with its bustling markets, intricate architecture, and rich cultural scene. Visit the

sprawling Jemaa el-Fnaa square, take a guided tour of the stunning Bahia Palace, and indulge in traditional Moroccan cuisine.

4. **Bali, Indonesia** - This lush, tropical paradise is a must-visit for those looking to escape the hustle and bustle of everyday life. Relax on the beaches of Seminyak, explore the rice terraces of Ubud, and immerse yourself in the island's rich spiritual heritage.

5. **Rio de Janeiro, Brazil** - This lively city is home to some of the world's most iconic landmarks, such as the Christ the Redeemer statue and the Sugarloaf Mountain, and is known for its legendary Carnival celebration.

6. **New York City, USA** - The city that never sleeps is a must-visit for anyone who wants to experience the energy, culture, and diversity that the United States has to offer. Visit the top of the Empire State Building, stroll through Central Park, and get tickets to a Broadway show.

7. **Rome, Italy** - This ancient city is a treasure trove of art, architecture, and history. Visit the Colosseum, marvel at the intricate mosaics of the Vatican Museums, and indulge in delicious Italian cuisine.

8. **Sydney, Australia** - With its stunning beaches, world-class restaurants, and vibrant cultural scene, Sydney is a must-visit for anyone looking for a modern, cosmopolitan experience. Visit the iconic Sydney Opera House, take a stroll through the Royal Botanic Garden, and explore the trendy neighborhoods of Surry Hills and Darlinghurst.

9. **Iceland** - This rugged, otherworldly destination is a must-visit for anyone who appreciates nature and adventure. Hike through the stunning landscapes of Vatnajökull National Park, relax in the hot springs of the Blue Lagoon, and witness the magical Northern Lights.

10. **Cape Town, South Africa** - This lively city is a melting pot of cultures, surrounded by some of the most breathtaking natural scenery in the world. Visit the top of Table Mountain, explore the vibrant neighborhoods of Bo-Kaap and Woodstock, and take a guided tour of the historic Robben Island.

These are just a few of the amazing destinations that every woman should experience around the world. So pack your bags, grab your passport, and get ready to embark on the adventure of a lifetime!

Traveling domestically can be just as exciting and enriching as traveling internationally. There are many different places to visit in the United States, and each one has its own unique experiences and attractions.

Here are my picks for the Top 10 Places Every Woman Should Visit in the US:

1. **New York City, NY** - Yes, New York City made it to both lists. That's how much I love it!

2. **San Francisco, CA** - This iconic city is renowned for its hilly streets, the famous Golden Gate Bridge, and bohemian culture. Visit the top of the Twin Peaks, explore the quirky neighborhoods of Haight-Ashbury and the Mission, and indulge in delicious seafood at Fisherman's Wharf.

3. **Miami, FL** - This vibrant city is a must-visit for anyone looking to soak up the sun, enjoy world-class dining, and experience the spirited energy of South Beach. Take a stroll along Ocean Drive, visit the colorful street art of Wynwood, and indulge in the city's famous Cuban cuisine.

4. **Washington, D.C.** - The nation's capital is home to some of the most iconic landmarks in the country, including the Lincoln Memorial, the Washington Monument, and the National Mall. Visit the Smithsonian museums, take a tour of the White House, and admire the stunning architecture of the U.S. Capitol.

5. **Las Vegas, NV** - Anyone who loves the excitement of a casino, the thrill of the strip, and the indulgence of high-end dining and shopping should visit this neon-lit city. See a show at one of the many theaters, hit the slots at one of the many casinos, and marvel at the breathtaking Fountains of Bellagio.

6. **New Orleans, LA** - This lively city is renowned for its music, food, and laid-back lifestyle. Visit the iconic French Quarter, take in a jazz performance

on Bourbon Street, and indulge in the city's famous Cajun and Creole cuisine.

7. **Denver, CO** - This mountain city is a must-visit for anyone who loves the great outdoors, craft beer, and a vibrant cultural scene. Take a scenic drive through the Rockies, sample the wares of one of the many local breweries, and visit the Denver Art Museum.

8. **Austin, TX** - This quirky city is known for its live music, laid-back lifestyle, and vibrant food scene. Explore the bustling neighborhoods of South Congress and East Austin, get tickets for the famous Austin City Limits Music Festival, and indulge in delicious Tex-Mex cuisine.

9. **Chicago, IL** - This vibrant city is renowned for its architecture, food, and cultural scene. Take a tour of the Willis Tower, stroll along the lakefront, and visit the Art Institute of Chicago. And don't forget to get a picture at The Bean!

10. **Los Angeles, CA** - This iconic city is home to some of the most famous landmarks and neighborhoods in the country, including Hollywood, Sunset Boulevard, and the Walk of Fame. Visit the Hollywood Hills, take a tour of the famous studios, and indulge in the city's diverse food scene.

These are just a few of the amazing destinations within the United States that every woman should experience.

Hack Your Travel

Traveling can be fun and educational, but it can also be expensive and take up a lot of time. Here are some of my favorite travel hacks that can help you save time and money on your next adventure:

1. **Use airline price tracking tools** - You can sign up for alerts on websites such as Kayak or Hopper to receive notifications when the price of a flight you're interested in changes. This can help you find the best deals on flights.

2. **Book flights on weekdays** - Airlines often offer lower prices on flights that depart on weekdays as opposed to weekends. So if you have flexibility with your

travel dates, try to book your flight for a Tuesday or a Wednesday.

3. **Consider alternative airports** - If you're flying to a major city, consider flying into a smaller airport nearby. It may be a bit further away from your final destination, but the cost savings can be substantial.

4. **Pack strategically** - Save money and space by packing multi-purpose items such as a scarf that can also be used as a blanket or a shirt that can be dressed up or down. Also, consider packing items like a universal adapter and travel-sized toiletries to save money on these items at your destination.

5. **Use public transportation** - The price of taxis and rideshare services can add up quickly, so consider using public transportation instead. Not only will you save money, but you'll also get a glimpse into the local culture and way of life.

6. **Be mindful of meal times** - Eating out three times a day can get expensive quickly, so consider eating breakfast and lunch at local cafes and markets and reserving dining at a restaurant for dinner. Also, research local food markets where you can pick up snacks and drinks to take with you throughout the day.

7. **Take advantage of free activities** - Many cities offer free or low-cost activities, such as outdoor concerts, museum admissions, and events at public parks. Do some research before your trip and plan to participate in as many free activities as possible.

8. **Book accommodations in advance** - If you know your travel dates, it's always best to book accommodations as far in advance as possible. Not only will you have a better chance of finding a place that fits your budget and preferences, but you'll also save money on last-minute rates.

9. **Research local promotions and discounts** - Many cities offer discounts and promotions to visitors, such as city passes and museum memberships. Do some research before your trip to see if there are any promotions that can help you save money.

10. **Keep an open mind** - The best part of traveling is experiencing new and exciting things, so try to keep an open mind and be spontaneous. You never

know what amazing experiences await you just around the corner.

With these hacks in your back pocket, you'll be able to travel like a pro and make the most of your adventures without breaking the bank!

Which Books Will You Take on Your Journey?

"The more that you read, the more things you will know. The more that you learn, the more places you'll go." —Dr. Seuss, "I Can Read With My Eyes Shut!"

Reading can be a valuable tool for personal growth and development, and there's no better way to expand your horizons and broaden your perspective than by reading books. Here are my top 10 books that I believe every young woman should read:

1. **"The Lean In Collection" by Sheryl Sandberg** - This book provides a roadmap for women looking to advance in their careers and helps women break down the barriers that hold them back.

2. **"The Power of Now" by Eckhart Tolle** - This book provides a simple yet profound explanation of how to live in the present moment and how this can help bring peace and happiness into our lives.

3. **"The 7 Habits of Highly Effective People"** by Stephen Covey - This book provides a practical framework for personal and professional success and teaches readers how to develop habits that will help them achieve their goals.

4. **"The Immortal Life of Henrietta Lacks"** by Rebecca Skloot - This non-fiction book tells the story of Henrietta Lacks, an African American woman whose cells were taken without her knowledge or consent and used to create one of the most important cell lines in medical history.

5. **"The Color Purple" by Alice Walker** - This book tells the story of a young

African American woman living in the rural south during the early 20th century and her journey towards self-discovery and empowerment.

6. **"The Handmaid's Tale" by Margaret Atwood** - This book takes place in a dystopian society where women are stripped of their rights and forced into sexual servitude. It serves as a warning against the erosion of women's rights and illustrates the dangers of a patriarchal society.

7. **"The Bell Jar" by Sylvia Plath** - This book is a powerful and moving account of a young woman's descent into mental illness and her journey toward recovery.

8. **"Little Women" by Louisa May Alcott** - This classic coming-of-age novel tells the story of four sisters growing up in the late 19th century and their journey toward adulthood.

9. "A Room of One's Own" by Virginia Woolf - This book is a groundbreaking work of feminist literature that argues for the importance of women's independence and the need for women to have their own space in which to create and pursue their passions.

10. **"The Adventures of Huckleberry Finn" by Mark Twain** - This classic novel tells the story of a young boy's journey down the Mississippi River and his encounters with racism and slavery. It provides a powerful commentary on the issues of its time and remains relevant to this day.

These books are not only fun to read, but they also make you think, teach valuable lessons and provide insights into what it's like to be human. I think every young woman can learn something from these books.

Watch a Movie on the Plane

"Movies are a machine that generates empathy." —Roger Ebert

Watching movies can be a great way to escape from reality, learn about different perspectives, and gain new insights. Here's my top 10 list of movies that every young woman should watch:

1. **"Hidden Figures"** - This movie tells the story of three African American women working as mathematicians at NASA during the Space Race and their fight for equality and recognition.

2. **"Erin Brockovich"** - This movie tells the true story of a single mother who takes on a powerful corporation and wins a landmark lawsuit on behalf of a small town that was poisoned by toxic chemicals.

3. **"The Devil Wears Prada"** - This movie explores the cutthroat world of high-fashion magazine publishing and the importance of finding a balance between work and personal life.

4. **"Thelma & Louise"** - This movie tells the story of two friends who embark on a road trip that turns into a journey of self-discovery and empowerment.

5. **"The Imitation Game"** - This movie tells the true story of mathematician and computer science pioneer Alan Turing and his work cracking the Nazi's Enigma code during World War II.

6. **"The Help"** - This movie explores the lives of African American maids working in homes in the segregated South and their relationship with the white women they work for.

7. **"Million Dollar Baby"** - This movie tells the story of a female boxer who trains with a grizzled veteran and the bond that develops between them.

8. **"The Iron Lady"** - This movie tells the story of former United Kingdom Prime Minister Margaret Thatcher's rise to power and her impact on politics both within the U.K. and globally.

9. **"Dead Poets Society"** - This movie tells the story of a high school English teacher who inspires his students to think outside the box and pursue their passions.

10. **"Bend It Like Beckham"** - This movie tells the story of a young woman from a traditional Indian family who dreams of playing professional soccer and the challenges she faces in pursuing her passion.

Most of these movies have strong, inspiring female characters and teach important lessons about sticking with something, being brave, and having determination. They also provide a unique look at the struggles and successes of women in different places and times.

Download the free Adulting Hard Workbook to use the "Movies to Watch" and "Books to Read" trackers. Just visit https://adultinghardbooks.com

CHAPTER NINE

FINDING YOUR TRIBE

"You're the average of the five people you spend the most time with." —Jim Rohn

L ET ME TELL YOU, making new friends as an adult is harder than trying to find your lost sock in the dryer! With our busy schedules and technology taking over, it's no wonder why it feels like it's harder than ever to connect with others these days.

But don't worry, I've got your back! I have some tried and true methods for finding your new BFFs.

Here are some ideas to help you find new friends:

1. **Online communities:** There are many websites and social media platforms that

allow you to connect with people who share your interests. Some popular ones include Meetup (www.meetup.com), Facebook groups, Reddit communities, and online forums.

2. **Interest-based clubs and organizations:** Join local groups and clubs that align with your hobbies and passions. You can find them by searching online or asking at local community centers.

3. **Volunteer work:** Give back to your community by volunteering for a cause you care about. This is a great way to meet new people who share your values and interests.

4. **Classes and workshops:** Take a class or attend a workshop on something you're interested in. You'll have the opportunity to meet new people and learn something new at the same time.

5. **Sports and fitness groups:** Join a local sports team or fitness group to stay active and meet new people.

6. **Travel:** Travel is a great way to meet new people and expand your social circle. Consider joining a travel group or taking a solo trip to a new destination.

7. **Professional networks:** Attend industry events and conferences to connect with people in your field. You can also join professional organizations to network with like-minded individuals.

8. **Mutual friends:** Ask your existing friends if they know anyone they could introduce you to. Mutual friends can be a great way to build new connections.

9. **Mastermind groups:** These are groups of like-minded individuals who come together to support each other in reaching their goals. Not only will you find new friends, but you'll also gain a whole group of accountability partners.

Remember, finding new friends takes time and effort, but the rewards are well worth it. So go ahead and try some of these ideas and see what works best for you!

· · · ● ● · ● · ● · · ·

Nurture Your Friendships

Just like any other relationship, a friendship requires effort and attention to maintain. That's why it's important to follow some basic rules of friendship if you want your relationship to be strong and lasting.

Here are some friendship dos and don'ts:

Dos:

Do listen: Give your full attention when your friend is speaking, and show empathy and understanding.

Do make time for your friend: Schedule regular catch-ups and make an effort to stay in touch.

Do be honest: Be truthful and open with your friend, but always do so with kindness and respect.

Do celebrate your friend's successes: Be their biggest cheerleader and show genuine excitement for their accomplishments.

Do offer support: Be there for your friend when they need you, and offer your help and advice when asked.

Don'ts:

Don't gossip: Keep confidential information to yourself and avoid spreading rumors.

Don't be unreliable: Follow through on plans and commitments, and don't cancel at the last minute.

Don't be judgmental: Respect your friend's opinions and decisions even if you don't agree with them.

Don't play the blame game: Take responsibility for your actions and avoid blaming others for problems.

Don't compare your friendship with others': Each friendship is unique and special in its own way.

· · · ● · ● · · ·

Emotional Intelligence

Emotional intelligence is also an important aspect of friendship. It involves the ability to understand, manage, and express your own emotions as well as understand and positively impact the emotions of others. Here are some tips to develop your emotional intelligence:

Practice self-awareness: Reflect on your emotions and how they impact your thoughts and behaviors.

Practice empathy: Put yourself in someone else's shoes and try to understand their emotions and perspectives.

Manage your emotions: Learn to regulate your emotions and don't let them control you.

Communicate effectively: Express your emotions clearly and listen actively to others.

Build positive relationships: Cultivate healthy and supportive relationships with others, including your friends.

By following these tips, you can build strong and lasting friendships that bring joy and happiness to your life.

• • • ● • ● • ● • •

You Are So Entertaining!

Entertaining friends at home is a great way to bond and create memories. It's also a fantastic opportunity to showcase your culinary skills and your personal style. Here are some recommendations to help you plan a successful get-together at your place and adult like a boss!

- **Plan the menu:** Consider your guests' dietary restrictions and preferences and plan a menu that everyone will enjoy. Make sure to have a good balance of sweet and savory options as well as drinks.

When entertaining friends, it's important to choose appetizers and dishes that are both delicious and easy to prepare. Here are some recommendations:

- Bruschetta - A simple appetizer made with sliced bread, garlic, tomatoes, and basil.

- Deviled eggs - Boiled eggs filled with a creamy mixture of mayonnaise, mustard, and spices.

- Baked Brie - A soft cheese baked in puff pastry and served with crackers or bread.

- Spinach and artichoke dip - A creamy dip made with spinach, artichokes, and cheese, served with chips or bread.

- Stuffed mushrooms - Mushroom caps stuffed with a mixture of breadcrumbs, herbs, and cheese.

- Chicken wings - Fried or baked chicken wings tossed in a sauce of your choice.

- Sliders - Mini burgers served on small buns with toppings of your choice.

- Meatballs - Meatballs made with ground beef, pork, or turkey, served with a sauce.

- Tacos - Tacos filled with meats, cheeses, and toppings of your choice, served with tortilla chips.

- Pasta salad - A cold pasta salad made with cooked pasta, vegetables, and a dressing of your choice.

When planning a dinner party, it's also important to consider the dietary restrictions of your guests. Offer a mix of vegetarian and meat-based options, as well as gluten-free and dairy-free options, if necessary. With a little planning and work, you can throw a party that your friends will remember and enjoy.

- **Ask for help:** Don't be afraid to ask guests to bring a dish or drinks to share. This takes some of the pressure off you and allows everyone to contribute.

- **Set the mood:** Create a cozy and inviting atmosphere by lighting candles, turning off the overhead lights, and playing some background music.

- **Engage in conversation:** Make sure to engage in conversation with all your guests and encourage them to get to know each other. You can also plan games or activities that everyone can participate in.

- **Serve drinks:** If you are all of legal drinking age, have a variety of drinks available, such as wine, beer, cocktails, and non-alcoholic beverages.

- **Enjoy the moment:** Take a step back and enjoy the moment. Your guests are there to spend time with you, so relax and have a good time.

With these tips, you'll be well on your way to hosting a successful get-together at your place. So pop open a bottle of wine, put on some music, and get ready to entertain your friends!

Red, Red, Wine

Alright girl, let's talk about the vino. First off, let me start on a serious note. If you're underage, don't drink. It's not only illegal, but it can also harm your health. And if you do choose to drink, always do so responsibly and in moderation. Excessive drinking can lead to serious health problems and is never a good idea.

Now, onto the fun stuff! Learning about wine can be a delightful experience. There's something special about savoring a glass of your favorite vintage and discovering new flavors and aromas. It's like a taste of adventure! Wine pairing refers to the art of matching wine with food to enhance the flavors of both. When pairing wine with food, you want to consider the intensity, flavors, and textures of both the wine and the food. A good rule of thumb is to match the intensity of the wine with the intensity of the food. For example, a glass of full-bodied wine should be paired with a full-flavored dish, such as steak, and a light-bodied wine should be paired with a light-flavored dish, such as fish. With a little experimentation and knowledge, you can create unforgettable wine and food pairings.

Every woman should try a few classic wines at some point in their life. Here's my list of must-try wines:

1. **Chardonnay** - A full-bodied white wine known for its creamy and buttery flavors. It pairs well with seafood, poultry, and creamy pasta dishes.

2. **Pinot Noir** - A light-to medium-bodied red wine known for its bright fruit flavors and subtle tannins. It pairs well with salmon, duck, and mushroom dishes.

3. **Cabernet Sauvignon** - A full-bodied red wine known for its bold fruity flavors,

such as blackberries and black cherries, and strong tannins. It pairs well with steak, lamb, and strong-flavored cheeses.

4. **Sauvignon Blanc** - A crisp and zesty white wine known for its herbal and grassy flavors. It pairs well with salads, seafood, and goat cheese.

5. **Merlot** - A medium-bodied red wine known for its smooth and fruity flavors. It pairs well with chicken, pasta dishes, and mild cheeses.

6. **Riesling** - A sweet to semi-sweet white wine known for its floral and fruity flavors. It pairs well with spicy foods, fruit-based desserts, and Thai cuisine.

7. **Syrah/Shiraz** - A full-bodied red wine known for its bold and spicy flavors. It pairs well with barbecued meats, hearty stews, and strong-flavored cheeses.

8. **Zinfandel** - A full-bodied red wine known for its high alcohol content and bold, fruity flavors. It pairs well with spicy foods, grilled meats, and rich sauces.

9. **Rosé** - A light-bodied wine with a pink color, known for its bright and fruity flavors. It pairs well with salads, seafood, and warm weather.

10. **Sparkling wine** - A light-bodied wine with bubbles known for its festive and celebratory nature. It pairs well with appetizers, desserts, and special occasions.

So, grab a glass, find a cozy spot, and start your wine journey! Just remember to always drink responsibly and in moderation. Cheers!

Dazzle Them With Your Bartending Skills

Alrighty, let's get mixing! Just like with wine, it's important to remember to **drink responsibly and in moderation.**

Here's my list of the top ten cocktails every woman should try:

1. **Margarita** - Mix 2 oz tequila, 1 oz triple sec, 1 oz fresh lime juice, and salt the rim of the glass. Shake the ingredients with ice and serve on the rocks.

2. **Mojito** - Muddle mint leaves, lime juice, and sugar in a glass. Fill the glass with ice, add 2 oz rum, and top with soda water.

3. **Gin and Tonic** - Fill a glass with ice, add 2 oz gin, top with tonic water, and garnish with a lime wedge.

4. **Old Fashioned** - Mix 2 oz whiskey, a splash of bitters, a sugar cube, and a splash of water in a glass. Stir, add ice, and garnish with an orange slice and a cherry.

5. **Daiquiri** - Blend 2 oz rum, 1 oz fresh lime juice, and 1 oz simple syrup. Serve over ice.

6. **Bloody Mary** - Mix 2 oz vodka, 4 oz tomato juice, a splash of Worcestershire sauce, a pinch of salt and pepper, and a dash of hot sauce. Garnish with a celery stalk and a lemon wedge.

7. **Manhattan** - Mix 2 oz whiskey, 1 oz sweet vermouth, and a dash of bitters in a glass. Stir, add ice, and garnish with a cherry.

8. **Bellini** - Blend 1 oz peach puree and 4 oz Prosecco. Serve in a flute glass.

9. **Cosmopolitan** - Mix 2 oz vodka, 1 oz triple sec, 1 oz cranberry juice, and 1 oz fresh lime juice. Shake with ice and serve in a martini glass.

10. **French Martini** - Mix 2 oz vodka, 1 oz Chambord, and 1 oz pineapple juice. Shake with ice and serve in a martini glass.

So, grab your shaker and start mixing! Just remember to always drink responsibly and in moderation. Enjoy!

CHAPTER TEN

FINDING YOUR LIFE MATE

love

F INDING LOVE IN TODAY'S world can be a real challenge. It's like trying to find a needle in a haystack, except the needle is a decent human being and the haystack is a sea of catfishes, ghosts, and people who only want to hook up.

In previous decades, the biggest challenge was probably trying to sneak out to meet your crush without getting caught by your parents. Nowadays, good luck figuring out if your crush is even real, or if they're just a stock photo of a model that someone stole off the internet.

If you're a single young woman looking for love, you may be facing some of these challenges. It can be hard to sort through all the options and find someone who's actually a good match for you. But don't get discouraged! Just take it one step at a time, and try to have fun with it. You never know who you might meet or what kind of amazing adventure might come from it.

Where to Look for Your Mate

Finding a life partner can be a tumultuous journey, but here are some ideas to get started:

Try online dating:
Online dating has become a popular way for people to meet, and there are a variety of apps and websites to choose from. The best dating apps and sites will vary depending on what you're looking for in a relationship and your personal preferences. Here are some popular options:

- **Tinder** - A location-based app that allows users to swipe right on profiles they like and start chatting if there's a mutual match.

- **Bumble** - A dating app where women make the first move. It operates similarly to Tinder, but only women can start conversations with their matches.

- **Hinge** - A dating app that's marketed as the dating app designed to be deleted. It uses a more in-depth compatibility algorithm to match users based on common interests, shared values, and more.

- **Match** - A dating site that has been around since the mid-90s. It's known for its detailed profile creation process and for being one of the first online dating sites.

- **OkCupid** - A dating site that uses a unique algorithm to match users based on their answers to various questions.

- **HER** - A dating app for LGBTQ+ women and non-binary people.

These are just a few examples, and there are many other dating apps and sites available. It's important to do your research, read reviews, and choose a reputable site that fits your needs and preferences.

Get involved in social activities:
Join clubs or groups based on your interests, volunteer for causes you care about, and attend local events. You never know who you might meet, and you'll have something in common to talk about right away.

Ask friends and family for introductions:
If you know someone who is happy in their relationship, ask if they know anyone they could introduce you to. They might be able to set you up with someone who shares your interests and values.

• • • • • • • • • • •

Safety First

To stay safe when chatting with someone or meeting them in person for the first time, here are some tips:

- **Trust your instincts:** If something seems too good to be true or makes you feel uncomfortable, it's probably best to proceed with caution.

- **Take things slow:** Don't feel pressured to move too quickly. Get to know someone online or over the phone before meeting them in person.

- **Meet in a public place:** When you do decide to meet in person, make sure it's in a well-lit public place like a cafe or park.

- **Tell someone you trust:** Let a friend or family member know where you're going and who you're meeting and check in with them after.

Before meeting someone in person, it's important to ask questions to get to know them better and assess if they're a good match. Here are some suggestions:

- What are your hobbies and interests?

- What's your career or job?

- What are your goals and aspirations?

- What are your values and beliefs?

- What are you looking for in a relationship?

- What is your favorite book, movie, or TV show?

- How do you spend your weekends?

- What do you like to do for fun?

- What kind of music do you listen to?

- What is something you've always wanted to try?

By asking these questions, you can get a better sense of who the person is and if they might be a good match for you.

Watch Out for Red Flags

When chatting with or meeting someone for the first time, it's important to be aware of red flags that could indicate that the person may not be who they seem or that the relationship might not be healthy. Here are some red flags to look out for:

1. **Pressure to move too quickly:** If someone is trying to rush into a relationship or asking you to meet in person before getting to know you, this could be a red flag.

2. **Inconsistent or vague answers:** If the person's responses to your questions are inconsistent or vague, this could be a sign that they're hiding something or being deceptive.

3. **Requests for personal information:** If the person is asking for personal information, such as your address or financial information before you've even met in person, this is a red flag.

4. **Controlling behavior or jealousy:** If the person is trying to control your actions, monitor your movements, or becomes overly jealous, this could be a sign of an unhealthy relationship.

5. **Aggressive or threatening behavior:** If the person is acting aggressively or making threatening comments towards you or others, this is a serious red flag,

and you should take it seriously.

6. **Disrespect:** If the person is constantly belittling you, mocking you, or treating you with disrespect, this is not a healthy dynamic, and you should consider ending the relationship.

It's important to trust your instincts and be aware of any red flags. If something doesn't feel right, don't ignore it. It's always better to be safe than sorry.

• • • • •• • •• • •• •

Your First Date

For a first date, it's important to choose an activity that allows you to get to know each other in a relaxed and comfortable setting. Here are some ideas for a first date—and remember, it doesn't have to be the man's role to come up with something fun to do:

- **Coffee or drinks:** Meeting for coffee or drinks can be a great low-key way to ease into a first date and get to know each other.

- **Outdoor activity:** If the weather is nice, consider a first date that involves an outdoor activity, such as a hike, picnic, or bike ride.

- **Cultural outing:** Visit a museum, art gallery, or concert to explore your shared interests in culture.

- **Foodie fun:** If you both enjoy trying new restaurants and cuisines, why not make it a foodie adventure and try a new place together?

- **Volunteer:** If you're both interested in giving back, consider volunteering together at a local organization.

- **DIY workshop:** Learn something new and bond over a DIY workshop or cooking class.

- **Game night:** Test your skills and get to know each other's personalities over a game night, whether it be board games or video games.

Remember, the most important thing is to find an activity that you both enjoy and feel comfortable doing. And remember, the person who asks the other out doesn't have to bear all the responsibility for coming up with something fun to do. Both parties can contribute ideas and take turns planning dates.

· · · · ● · ● · ● · · ·

Fall Deep... Fall Hard

Falling in love can be an amazing experience. Key elements of a healthy, loving relationship include:

1. **Acceptance:** You feel like you can be yourself without fear of judgment or rejection.

2. **Trust:** You trust each other to be honest, reliable, and supportive.

3. **Communication:** You can openly and effectively communicate with each other.

4. **Mutual support:** You support each other's goals, dreams, and aspirations.

5. **Shared interests:** You have common interests and enjoy doing things together.

6. **Laughter:** You share a sense of humor and laugh together often.

7. **Physical affection:** You enjoy physical touch, such as holding hands, cuddling, and giving each other hugs.

To help a relationship last, it's important to develop a set of emotional and communication skills. Here's a list of skills every woman should have:

• **Active listening:** Intentionally paying attention to what your partner is saying and showing them that you're engaged in the conversation.

- **Empathy:** Being able to understand and share your partner's emotions and experiences.

- **Compromise:** Being willing to meet halfway and find solutions that work for both of you.

- **Conflict resolution:** Being able to calmly and respectfully handle disagreements and conflicts.

- **Positive communication:** Speaking kindly and positively to your partner, even during difficult conversations.

- **Patience:** Being willing to wait for your partner and allow time for things to develop.

- **Humor:** Using humor to lighten the mood and diffuse tense situations.

Practicing these skills can greatly improve the likelihood of having a lasting, fulfilling relationship. Just remember, love isn't always easy, but it's worth the effort to make it work! And don't forget, laughter is the best medicine, so don't be afraid to laugh with your partner and enjoy the journey.

Practice Nonviolent Communication

Nonviolent Communication (NVC) is a method of communication that focuses on empathy, understanding, and connection rather than criticism, blame, or judgment. It's based on the idea that every person has value and every person's needs are important. When we communicate using NVC, we're more likely to create positive and meaningful connections with others.

Here's how to practice NVC in a relationship:

1. **Observe without evaluation:** Observe the situation without making any judgments or assumptions about the other person's behavior.

2. **Feelings:** Identify and express your feelings about the situation.

3. **Needs:** Identify the underlying needs or values that aren't being met.

4. **Request:** Make a clear, specific, and non-threatening request to meet your needs.

Here's an example of NVC in action:

- You: *"When you came home late last night, I felt worried and scared."*

- Partner: *"I understand. I'm sorry I made you feel that way."*

- You: *"I have a need for safety and security in our relationship. Can we make a plan for you to let me know when you'll be home late in the future?"*

By using NVC, you can communicate your feelings and needs in a way that's non-threatening and respectful. This can lead to a deeper understanding and connection between partners.

If you'd like to learn more about NVC, you can check out the book "Nonviolent Communication: A Language of Life" by Marshall Rosenberg or visit the website www.cnvc .org. There are also many workshops and resources online that can help you learn NVC and how to use it in your relationships.

CONCLUSION

WELL, MY DEAR YOUNG woman, we've come to the end of our journey together, and what a journey it has been! You have learned that adulting is not a destination, it's a state of mind and a journey filled with laughter, tears, and a lot of "Aha!" moments.

We started by discussing the difference between being an adult and just getting older. Some young women grow up faster than others, and that's okay, but this book is specifically for the young woman who has been living life like it's golden, and now it's time to face reality. Don't worry, I've got your back.

Next, we tackled the daunting task of finding a place to call home, how to make it look like a palace with some decorating tips, and how to keep it running smoothly with basic repairs and home maintenance. And, of course, I made sure you wouldn't go hungry with some cooking tips, meal prep ideas, pantry essentials, and grocery shopping advice. You'll be the hostess with the mostest in no time!

We also talked about getting a sweet ride and keeping it sweet, because who wants to take the bus when you can have a car that says, "I've arrived"? And of course, I made sure to leave you with some self-grooming tips and advice on the most versatile outfits so that you can feel and look like a boss.

Moving on to the nitty-gritty of adulting, we covered the most important topic: money! You learned about job hunting, making money, budgeting, making big purchases, investing, and basic tax strategies. I made sure you were equipped with all the tools to handle your finances like a pro.

Next, we covered home safety tips, cybersecurity, avoiding scams, first aid, and how to live alone safely. Because safety always comes first.

I also made sure that you can take care of your mind and body with goal and vision setting, handling big emotions, dental and medical checkups, mindfulness, and understanding the health insurance system. And because I want you to be the most interesting woman in the world, I provided travel hacks, must-see destinations, books to read, and movies to watch. Don't forget to journal your experiences and create your bucket list.

Finally, we talked about finding your tribe, whether it's new friends, wine lovers, or the love of your life. I provided tips on how to find new friends, make the most of your relationships, and navigate the world of online and real-life dating.

So, in short, you have learned everything you need to know to be a kickass adult, and I'm so proud of you! Just remember, adulting can be tough, but it can also be a lot of fun. Keep smiling, keep laughing, and make sure to visit https://adultinghardbooks.com for more information and free resources. And with that, I say goodbye, for now. But remember, you're never really alone—I'll always be here for you. Happy adulting!

· · ● ◉ · ◉ ● · ·

Please Leave a Review

As an independent author, positive reviews can make or break my business.

If you got some value out of this book, please leave a great review. It will mean the world to me!

Thank you very much,

Jeff

ALSO BY JEFFREY C. CHAPMAN

Hello there! As an author, I know just how important reviews are for getting the word out about my work. When readers leave a review on Amazon, it helps others discover my book and decide whether it's right for them. Plus, it gives me valuable feedback on what readers enjoyed and what they didn't.

So if you've read my book and enjoyed it (or even if you didn't!), I would really appreciate it if you took a moment to leave a review on Amazon. It doesn't have to be long or complicated - just a few words about what you thought of the book would be incredibly helpful.

Thank you so much for your support!

Jeff

If you enjoyed this book, please check out:

Adulting Hard for Young Men

Adulting Hard in Your Late Twenties and Thirties

Adulting Hard After College

Made in the USA
Middletown, DE
22 May 2023

31169043R00106